"Whenever war existed between Great Britain and France, the province of New York was the principal theatre of colonial contest. It became the Flanders of America, and it had to sustain, from time to time, the scourge and fury of savage and Canadian devastation. We need only cast an eye upon our geographical position, and read the affecting details of the formidable expeditions, and the frightful incursions which laid waste our northern and western frontiers, between 1690, and the conquest of Canada, in 1760, to be deeply impressed with a sense of the difficulties which this colony had to encounter, and of the fortitude and perseverance with which they were overcome."

*James Kent, Chancellor of the State of New York
Anniversary Address before the
New-York Historical Society, December 6, 1828*

C O

Introduction	2
The French and Indian War 1754–1763	4
The Great Lakes Seaway Trail	**12**
Fort Le Boeuf	14
Fort de la Presque Île (Isle)	16
Old Fort Niagara	18
Fort Ontario State Historic Site (Oswego)	20
Fort de La Présentation	22
Fort Lévis	24
The Revolutionary Byway	**26**
Schenectady Stockade Historic District	28
Old Fort Johnson	30
Johnson Hall State Historic Site	32
Fort Klock Historic Restoration	34
Fort Stanwix National Monument	36
Fort Brewerton Blockhouse Museum	38
Lakes to Locks Passage	**40**
Crailo State Historic Site	42
Fort Edward and Rogers Island	44
Lake George Battlefield	46
Fort William Henry	48
Lake George Shipwrecks	50
Fort Carillon/Ticonderoga	52
Crown Point State Historic Site	54
Visitor Information and Resources	56
Timeline of the French and Indian War	Inside back cover

Introduction

For 150 years, culminating in the 1750s, the super-powers of the 18th century — France and Great Britain — contested for empire and the destiny of North America along a strategic triangle of waterways in today's New York State. The St. Lawrence and Mohawk rivers provided access to the heart of the continent from the Atlantic Ocean. North-south, the Hudson River/Lake George/Lake Champlain waterway linked the principal French and British trading centers — Montréal and Québec—with Albany and New York City, and with the interior.

The course of empire flowed along the waterways penetrating the North American continent. European kings sought to control the continent by controlling the waterways Indians had been using for trade and war for millennia. "The lakes and rivers are the only outlets, the only open roads in this country," observed a senior French officer. By the 1730s, after a generation of intensive construction on the frontiers, a ring of forts protected the water gateways to *la Nouvelle France* (New France): Louisbourg guarded the mouth of the St. Lawrence on the Atlantic Ocean; Niagara to the west controlled access to and from the Great Lakes; St-Frédéric at Crown Point protected the Lake Champlain portal to the south. Thomas Pownall, the royal governor of Massachusetts Bay observed:

> *The Waters in this Country hold the Imperium of it; . . . whoever are possessed of these Waters must command the Country. . . . The French by having Ticonderoga Oswego Niagara &c are in actual Possession of that Country . . . and Consequently Command the Service of the Indians. . . . They have an Easy & uninterrupted Communication to all their Posts & . . . many of these Posts [become] entrepôts for their Operations against us.*

As frontier tensions erupted once again into open warfare in the mid-1750s, old forts were strengthened and new, more distant, outposts nearer the enemy were built along these waterways. This is a multi-cultural story about the birth of nations: the United States, Canada, Britain, France, and numerous native nations. This is an international story, not merely a local or regional one. This was a world war. Here is where history in your own backyard dramatically becomes world history.

To ensure that a new generation discovers this significant chapter in the founding of our nation, the New York State Legislature created in 2004 a French & Indian War 250th Anniversary Commemoration Commission to create a series of re-enactment experiences between 2005 and 2010 which could provide "time-machine" portals into the world of the 1750s. In addition, the Commission has developed educational programming, historical publications, tourism promotion, and other commemorative events to reach families and classrooms across the land.

This shared story of nation-building still survives on a nearby frontier — just a few days' march away! We appreciate your support of this effort to reintroduce Americans and Canadians to the birth-pangs of our nations. We applaud your commitment to our shared history. Now enjoy the discoveries that await you!

On behalf of the Commission,
and in memory of those who made the Empire State hallowed ground 250 years ago,

Nicholas Westbrook
Vice Chair, NYS French & Indian War
250th Anniversary Commemoration Commission
and Director Emeritus, Fort Ticonderoga

French siege gun c. 1750.

The French and Indian War 1754–1763

Water was the lifeblood, the circulatory system for the French and Indian War. Locating the names of the major battles of the war on a map of the northeastern quadrant of North America at the middle of the 18th century places every major confrontation on, or adjacent to, bodies of water. Battles of Lake George, Fort William Henry, Fort Carillon, Fort St. Frédéric, Fort Niagara, Fort Frontenac, Fort Ontario (Oswego), Louisbourg, Québec, and Montréal, are inextricably linked to Lakes Champlain, George, and Ontario and the St. Lawrence River. Other waterways served as feeders, sources of men and material.

The war in North America began with a dispute over the construction of a fort at the confluence of three rivers in western Pennsylvania — the Allegheny, the Monongahela, and the Ohio. It ended six years later at Montréal on the St. Lawrence River. That much of the fighting between those two events took place in and around the colony of New York is not surprising. A second look at the same map reveals yet another striking feature, the geometry of New York's waterways, which helps explain the colony's attraction to military strategists. Three water routes dominate the landscape, forming the sides of a triangle — the Mohawk River Valley, connecting Albany and the Hudson River through Lake Oneida to Lake Ontario; the Lake Ontario to Montréal stretch of the St. Lawrence River; and the Lake George/Lake Champlain corridor connecting the Hudson River to Montréal via the Richelieu River. Men, arms, and supplies that flowed back and forth along those three arteries as armies in the thousands jockeyed for position. Noteworthy, as well, is that the major battles of the French and Indian War for the most part cluster around the vertices of that triangle and that the culminating campaign against Montréal, which brought the war to an end, utilized all three legs of the triangle — one for supply and two for attack. Control of the water meant control of the war.

Waterways of War introduces three Byway routes corresponding to the three legs of the New York waterway triangle. Lakes to Locks Passage takes the traveler to key sites along the Albany-to-Montréal route, the Great Lakes Seaway Trail links Montréal and Lake Ontario, continuing through Niagara and Lake Erie to the Presque Île (Isle)/Fort Le Boeuf portage in Western Pennsylvania, and the Revolutionary Byway includes sites along the Lake Ontario-to-Albany connection. Accessing the Byway system at any point and making a complete circuit of the 19 sites described in the following pages would be not only a trip through the bewitching landscape of upstate New York and Pennsylvania, but a journey through time to the 18th century, thrusting the visitor into the heart of the French and Indian War. Do part of it. Do all of it. Learn. Enjoy!

French cannon barrel c. 1750.

By 1750, the stage was set for a major confrontation in North America between France and Britain. The period of exploration of the lands east of the Mississippi was long over. For more than one hundred-forty years the two European powers had been staking out their respective claims to territory in the New World. In 1607 England had established its first permanent settlement in North America at Jamestown, Virginia. After several voyages exploring the Northeast coast in the vicinity of the mouth of the St. Lawrence River, Samuel de Champlain returned in 1608 with a group of fur traders to establish a French settlement at Québec. From then until the middle of the 18th century, the English spread north along the seacoast, in the process swallowing Swedish and Dutch colonies, until they inhabited the entire coastal plain from Maine to Georgia between the Atlantic Ocean and the Appalachian Mountains. The French, meanwhile, were moving down the St. Lawrence Valley into the Great Lakes and were spreading into the interior of the continent between the Mississippi River and the Appalachians.

Between 1689 and 1748 the two countries fought three separate wars in Europe, each of which had spilled over into North America — King William's War (1689–1697), Queen Anne's War (1701–1713), and King George's War (1744–1748). As the English population increased along the Atlantic coast and began looking for room to expand beyond the Appalachians, and as conflicting British and French claims began to overlap, the time inevitably arrived when France and Britain would face

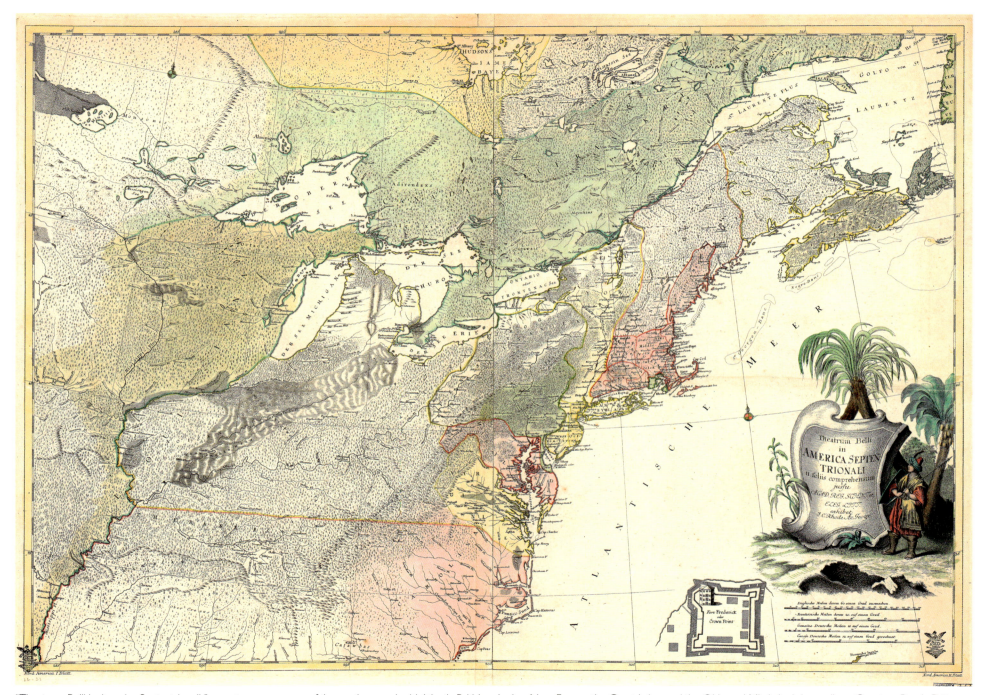

"Theatrum Belli in America Septentrionali," a contemporary map of the northern and mid-Atlantic British colonies, New France, the Great Lakes and the Ohio and Mississippi river valleys. Courtesy Randy Patten.

off directly over their possessions in America. This was to be a war with far-reaching geographic implications — it has sometimes been described, most notably by Winston Churchill, as the first "world war." Fighting would occur in Europe, in the Caribbean, and even in Asia. Much of the fighting, however, was destined to take place in the northeastern portion of the North American continent, thousands of miles from the home countries of the principal combatants, in a region where an indigenous population already thrived.

Frequently overlooked in narratives of the fighting between the armies of these European foes were the tragic consequences for the North American native peoples struggling to maintain their lands, their identities, and their traditional ways of life against the alien pressures of Western progress and an emerging global economic system. The very name most often used in America to characterize this conflict — the French and Indian War — is an Anglo-American distortion of what took place. Too often people accept as fact the oversimplification that on one side were the British and on the other the French and their Indian allies. Too often we forget that the British forces consisted of three distinct elements — the European British, the provincial British colonists, and the most cohesive of the native units, the Iroquois. Shifting alliances among Indian tribes and both the French and English, neither of whom made best use of their Indian allies, would play a significant role in the bitter and complex struggle to dominate the North American continent.

Beginnings

The immediate cause of the war was the determination of the European rivals to establish control over what was known as the Ohio Country, that area of western Pennsylvania centering around the Forks of the Ohio, where the Allegheny River flowing south and the Monongahela River flowing north meet to form *La Belle Rivière*, the Ohio River. Control of this strategically important piece of real estate would determine control of the entire territory along the Ohio on its course to the Mississippi. The British needed land. The French were intent on maintaining an unbroken line of communication between Montréal and their possessions in Louisiana, particularly New Orleans. Indians near the Forks, among them the Shawnees and Delawares, many of whom had migrated to the region from coastal communities under pressure from the mushrooming English population along the Atlantic, were wooed by both sides. Having greater fear of the English intent to settle and develop, which would drive Indian tribes even deeper into the continent, most favored the French, who did not seem so concerned about appropriating their lands. Further complicating the situation was the resentment harbored by many of these Ohio tribes against the six tribes of the Iroquois League, whose concentration of power, while maintaining close ties to the British, enabled them to treat other Native Americans as subject peoples.

By 1753, the French had begun constructing a series of forts south from Lake Erie which would culminate in the establishment of a fort at the Forks giving them control of the Ohio Valley now claimed by the French, the British, the Iroquois, and the Ohio Mingos, an offshoot of the Senecas. Governor Dinwiddie of Virginia sent an envoy demanding that the French withdraw; the French refused. In January, the English began erecting a fort of their own at the Forks. The French responded with a show of force under Captain Claude-Pierre Pécaudy de Contrecoeur in April which convinced the British construction crew under Ensign Edward Ward to depart quietly. (Ward even sold Contrecoeur his tools!) The French completed the construction of Fort Duquesne; Governor Dinwiddie sent out a detachment of troops under the command of the young George Washington to harass the French; an encounter in the wilderness ensued; shots were exchanged; and, once order was seemingly restored, the wounded French commander, Joseph Coulon de Villiers de Jumonville, was killed by a hatchet blow to the skull. The complexities of the network of relationships among the French, British colonists, and Indians were all wrapped up in the figure of Tanaghrisson, the wielder of the hatchet and murderer of

A 19th-century engraving of George Washington and Christopher Gist on their mission to Ft. Le Boeuf in December, 1753.

A British plan of Fort Duquesne c. 1756.

Jumonville. Tanaghrisson was known as "the Half-King," a Seneca assigned by the Iroquois to represent the Ohio Indians, an ambiguous role at best. Having recently lost his status with his French-leaning charges, Tanaghrisson's dramatic blow was a desperate attempt to restore his personal authority and, by extension, the authority of the Iroquois, over neighboring subordinate tribes. It was an attempt that ultimately failed. Blood had been spilled. A threshold had been crossed. Although there were no immediate declarations of war, a conflict that was to grow and spill across the civilized world had been ignited in the backwoods of Pennsylvania.

Advantage to the French

The next several years were not kind to the British. Following the firefight at what came to be known as Jumonville's Glen, Washington stubbornly moved forward to attack Fort Duquesne with inadequate troops and materials and without Indian support. Warned of the arrival of a sizeable French and Indian force, he retreated to a poorly-sited, hastily-constructed Fort Necessity where on July 3 he suffered a humiliating defeat, signing surrender documents in which he admitted to the "assassination" of Jumonville. Both sides then pulled back to lick their wounds and draft campaign plans for the following year.

Early 1755 saw the arrival of regular army forces under new leadership from both France and Britain. Marquis de Vaudreuil was named Governor-General of Canada and given overall authority for managing the conflict with Britain in North America. Jean-Armand, Baron de Dieskau, was named commander of the French forces, but was responsible to Vaudreuil. The British took a different approach, giving Major General Edward Braddock control, not only over military affairs, but, in response to the inability of the colonies to work together constructively, authority over the colonial governments as well. Braddock, arrogant and dismissive of both provincial soldiers

The war at sea

Both Great Britain and France had overseas colonies around the world — in North America, the Caribbean, Africa and Asia, and both maintained large navies to protect maritime commerce in times of peace and support land operations in time of war.

To Great Britain, the Royal Navy was of the utmost importance, not least in defending the island nation against possible invasion — always a threat in time of war. France, as a major land power, needed a large army in Europe, and the navy, while strong, was usually of secondary importance.

Access to the heart of New France was by way of the St. Lawrence River, and England's navy could readily intercept French shipping entering or leaving this waterway. France's fortress of Louisbourg was built as a secure naval base for French warships, but its capture by Amherst in July 1758 left New France completely exposed to British seapower, choking off reinforcements and supplies from France.

The campaigns against Québec in 1759 and against Montréal in 1760 were enabled largely by the power of the Royal Navy to bring troops and supplies unopposed up the St. Lawrence river. Britain also waged a successful naval campaign in the Caribbean, capturing French-owned islands whose sugar production was of enormous economic value, more than New France itself.

In 1756, Admiral John Byng commanded Britain's Mediterranean fleet. In a confused series of actions, Byng's hesitancy resulted in the loss of British-held Minorca, an important naval base. Public outcry led to Byng's court-martial and eventual execution in 1757. French philosopher Voltaire wrote mockingly "that in this country (England) it is a good thing to kill an admiral from time to time *pour encourager les autres*" — to encourage the others!

One of the most smashing naval victories of the war was won by British Admiral Sir Edward Hawke at Quiberon Bay off the coast of France on November 20, 1759, over French Admiral Conflans's fleet, which ended any threat of a French invasion of England.

Britain's strong naval traditions and sizable fleets of warships and merchant ships generally gave her the upper hand in most naval or maritime operations undertaken during the Seven Years' War. RT

During the siege of Louisbourg in 1758, two 74-gun French warships were "cut out" — captured by British sailors and marines attacking in small boats, in this case under heavy fire from the fort. The *Prudente* ran aground and was burnt, but the *Bienfaisant* was safely brought away. Image courtesy Ron Toelke.

and Indian allies, was killed at the beginning of July in a disastrous encounter with French and Indian forces near Fort Duquesne in a battle that demonstrated the folly of using conventional European tactics in a wilderness setting. Fleeing not only the field of battle, but the entire Pennsylvania frontier, British troops sought shelter in Philadelphia where, even though it was mid-July, they insisted upon winter quarters. The Ohio Country having been abandoned to the French and their Indian allies, giving them free rein to launch devastation on the widely scattered and unprotected settlements, refugees began pouring into the coastal communities, and the focus of the fighting shifted into the north country.

The war in North America consisted primarily of three fronts — the Ohio Country which encompassed the frontier portions of Virginia and Pennsylvania, the Gulf of St. Lawrence and the lower part of that river valley, and the upstate New York-St. Lawrence waterways. And it was waterways that were the key. Unencumbered soldiers could make relatively good time by land, but the thick woodlands of the Northeast dictated that roads had to be cut through the forests for artillery and supplies to accompany those troops, essential adjuncts for a successful campaign. The armies of the French and Indian War therefore utilized, whenever possible, river and lake routes to move forces efficiently.

Of particular concern to the British was the French fortress at Louisbourg, captured by New England colonial forces in 1745, but returned to France, to the disgust of New Englanders, as part of the Treaty of Aix-la-Chapelle ending King George's War in 1748. Situated on Île Royale (now Cape Breton Island), Louisbourg provided protection for French ships entering the St. Lawrence, and its removal became a primary objective for the British. Denying access to the St. Lawrence would effectively shut off Canada's only outside source of arms, men, and supplies.

1755 saw the capture of Forts Beauséjour and Gaspereau on the isthmus connecting Nova Scotia and the Canadian mainland. Nova Scotia had been under control of the British, but with a large population of Acadians sympathetic to Canada, the capture of the forts effectively shut off overland contact between Québec and Louisbourg, setting the stage for a future siege of Louisbourg. To ensure complete control, English forces initiated a process of "ethnic cleansing", deporting thousands of Acadians over the next few years to mainland English colonies. It was this enforced deportation that brought Acadian, or "Cajun" culture to the bayou country of Louisiana.

September, 1755, also saw the collision of French and British forces in the Battle of Lake George, later claimed as an English victory, but inconclusive at best. Following that clash, the French began construction of Fort Carillon at Ticonderoga, and the English erected Fort William Henry near the site of the battle.

In the early months of 1756, new leadership arrived from Europe in the form of the Marquis de Montcalm for the French and John Campbell, fourth Earl of Loudoun for the English. Both appointments created complications for their country's respective war efforts. Montcalm clashed with Governor Vaudreuil over fundamentals of war strategy, and their bitter rivalry would eventually compromise French efforts. Loudoun clashed with royal governors and their legislatures, alienating colonists and making it extremely difficult to cultivate the support that he required. London and Versailles (the huge palace complex outside Paris that was the seat of the French government), meanwhile, faced the breakdown of diplomacy in Europe, resulting finally in mutual declarations of war in May. Military activity in 1756 in North America produced one major engagement when Montcalm captured and destroyed the British forts on Lake Ontario at the mouth of the Oswego River.

In 1757 successes continued to pile up for the French, with the most significant prize the capture of Fort William Henry in August. The ensuing chaotic massacre, by Indians denied their plunder, of the wounded and of other paroled British soldiers returning to Fort Edward demonstrated just how little control the European leadership exerted on their Indian allies. The confused aftermath of this battle also marked the withdrawal of the Indians as effective allies to the French in the northern theater of operations. Disappointed by the unfulfilled promises of the French command and struck down by a smallpox epidemic spread through blankets and clothing in captured British supplies, the Indians from the *pays d'en haut*, that Canadian territory surrounding and extending north and west from the Great Lakes, retreated into their homelands for the duration of the war.

An 18th-century French print depicting an Iroquois warrior.

British Rebound

Abrupt changes in British policy in 1758 resulted in improved fortunes for the British. Recognizing the imperative for colonial support, the new Prime Minister William Pitt recalled Lord Loudoun and reversed several of his most objectionable practices. Provincial officers would no longer be subordinate to any regular officer, but only to officers of equal or greater rank. Colonial legislatures would no longer be required to raise and utilize their own money for their defense, but would be reimbursed by the British government. Colonies which had continually resisted involvement and had provided little support now met or exceeded their manpower quotas with ease. Colonists now began to see themselves not as bullied participants, but as valued partners. James Abercromby replaced Lord Loudoun, but without his civilian authority, which remained in the hands of Pitt. Jeffery Amherst, James Wolfe, and George Augustus, Lord Howe were promoted to commands of great responsibility. British troops adopted more appropriate techniques for fighting in the wilderness.

The first efforts of the new leadership were not encouraging. An attempt to capture Fort Carillon in early July failed dismally, a result of poor judgment on the part of Abercromby and the death of the popular and innovative Lord Howe. Montcalm, however, had little time to savor his victory. News followed shortly of the fall of the fortress at Louisbourg after a 48-day siege, and the surrender, after only a two-hour bombardment, of Fort Frontenac, the heart of France's supply and trading operations in the Great Lakes.

Victorious French troops salute Montcalm after the defeat of Abercromby's British army in July, 1758. Painting by Henry A. Ogden, 1930, courtesy Fort Ticonderoga Museum.

Autumn saw yet another important victory for the British on the Pennsylvania frontier. The Ohio Indian tribes, concerned with the decline in the ability of the French to provide them with either adequate protection or trade goods, agreed in the Treaty of Easton to stand aside as the British advanced on a weakened Fort Duquesne. Faced with certain defeat, the French abandoned the fort, blowing it up on their way out. Events had turned completely against the French, the string of British victories in 1758 indicative of things to come.

The poor showing of the French military in 1758 unfortunately coincided with near famine in the Canadian winter of 1758–1759. Poor harvests in 1756 and 1757 were only compounded by the increasing

The scale of Britain's effort against Carillon in 1758 is evident in Frederick Coffay Yohn's painting titled "Embarkation of Abercromby's Expedition, July, 1758." The great number of boats and bateaux needed to move such a large force covered Lake George for miles. Courtesy Chapman Historical Museum.

A provincial soldier at war

David Wooster was born in Stratford, Connecticut in 1711. A Yale graduate in 1738, he served as a lieutenant in 1739 and was a captain of provincials at the capture of Louisbourg in 1745. Wooster's distinguished service made him a favorite of King George II and gained him a captain's commission in Sir William Pepperell's Regiment of regulars.

During the French and Indian War he was colonel of the 3rd Connecticut Regiment of provincials, and was with Abercromby's army at Carillon in 1758, and with Amherst's army that advanced to Canada in 1759. Wooster ended the war as a colonel commanding a brigade in 1763.

A major general of Connecticut militia at the start of the Revolution in 1775, Wooster was made a brigadier general in the new Continental army. He was with Gen. Richard Montgomery's invasion of Canada, taking command when Montgomery was killed in the failed attack on Québec in December, 1775. Wooster organized resistance to the large British raid on Danbury in April 1777. He was mortally wounded in the fighting and died in Danbury on May 2, 1777.
RT

General David Wooster c. 1775.

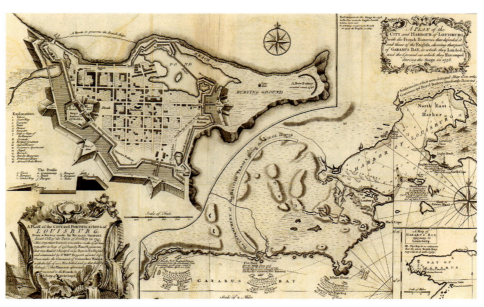

"A plan of the city and harbour of Louisburg with the French batteries that defended it and those of the English, shewing that part of Gabarus Bay in which they landed, and the ground on which they encamped during the siege in 1758." This map shows the extent of the powerful Louisbourg fortifications as well as details related to the 1758 siege. Courtesy of Cartography Associates, The David Rumsey Collection.

ability of the British navy to prevent supply ships from reaching New France, and there were fewer of those. Military stores were increasingly being diverted to French troops fighting in Europe. For Versailles, the war that had started in the back woods of Pennsylvania was taking a back seat to the more immediate fighting on the European continent, which did not bode well for the French forces in America.

In early May, Montcalm received news from Versailles that his dispute with Vaudreuil had been resolved in his favor. No longer would Vaudreuil's belief in the effectiveness of Indian allies and French woodsmen engaging in the hit-and-run tactics of guerilla warfare dictate operational thinking. Montcalm, who all along had wanted to conduct a European-style defensive campaign based on massed troops meeting on a field of battle, would now be in charge. Reining in his far-flung troops, he contracted the field of operations, concentrating his troops at Québec, preparing to take on the British in a terrain more to his liking.

Britain's grand strategic blueprint for a 1759 three-pronged attack on Montréal and Québec did not come to pass. Original plans had called for General Prideaux to take Fort Niagara and then move down the St. Lawrence, meeting Amherst's forces as they moved in from the Lake George-Lake Champlain-Richelieu River corridor. With Prideaux's death at Niagara, his replacement Sir William Johnson, an experienced provincial field commander, decided that his army had accomplished enough in securing control of the Great Lakes for the British and cutting off communication between

"The Death of General Wolfe" by Benjamin West painted in 1770. West's dramatic composition is nonetheless accurate in its depiction of uniforms, weapons and the setting of the bloody battlefield before the walls of Québec. Courtesy Wikimedia Commons.

New France's headquarters on the St. Lawrence and the western forts, now rendered relatively impotent. Amherst met little resistance on his passage through Lakes George and Champlain as Montcalm pulled his forces back to protect Québec. Preferring to consolidate his position in the lakes region, the better to defend against a possible Montcalm offensive should Wolfe fail in his attempt to take Québec, Amherst decided not to continue on to Montréal. That left Wolfe and his expeditionary naval force to carry out the conquest of the St. Lawrence.

After probing Québec's defenses for two months, which included ruinous shelling of the city itself and the complete destruction of the surrounding farmlands and communities in an effort to draw Montcalm's defenders out from the city, Wolfe landed two thousand men at the foot of a narrow path which took them up 175-foot-tall cliffs just west of the city. Emerging from the climb onto the Plains of Abraham outside the city walls, the British assumed battle positions, spreading out in a line two-deep across the mile-wide expanse. Confronted with this unexpected apparition, Montcalm felt he had no choice but to engage the attacking army. In a brief fifteen-minute battle, the better-trained and better-disciplined British routed the French. Montcalm and Wolfe both died as a result of wounds received during the fighting, and the remaining French army fled to the safety of Montréal, New France's sole remaining bastion.

Checkmate

British plans for 1760 mirrored those for 1759, but this time each of the expeditions that constituted the three-pronged attack on Montréal succeeded. Warships under General James Murray sailed up the St. Lawrence to Montréal, Amherst arrived from the opposite direction leading a force of eleven thousand down the St. Lawrence from Oswego, and a third contingent of thirty-five hundred under General William Haviland approached from the south along the Lake Champlain-Richelieu River route. Despite resistance from the French under the command of a stubborn General François-Gaston de Lévis, Montréal was forced to capitulate on September 8, 1760.

With the cessation of hostilities and the eventual implementation of the terms of the peace treaty signed on February 10, 1763, an astonishing transformation of the North American continent had taken place. The French, who had controlled so much territory, were effectively banished, retaining only the small islands of St. Pierre and Miquelon as fishing bases giving them access to the Grand Banks. The Indians, whether having allied themselves with the French or the British, found themselves to have gained nothing except empty promises. Unrelenting pressures of an expanding population and the attraction of rich lands beyond the Appalachians could not be checked. Amherst, given the job of administering the newly acquired territories, made no effort to honor the promises made to Native Americans, and white settlers swarmed across the Appalachians. Even George Washington, newly land-rich after having acquired thousands of acres as reward for his service to Virginia, acknowledged that promises made to Indians were nothing more than temporary expedients made to bring them into line. The British, previously confined to a relatively narrow strip along the coast, were suddenly faced with managing what would prove to be an unmanageable landscape and a freshly energized population extending from Canada to Georgia and from the Atlantic Ocean to the Mississippi River. ■ SB

Living history and battle reenactment events at many Byway historic sites bring the French and Indian War period to life for today's visitors. Here, reenactors, many from Québec, portray French regulars and *compagnies franche de la marine* at the 250th anniversary commemorative event at Lake George Battlefield in July 2005. Photo courtesy Randy Patten.

The cost of empire

1763 found Great Britain in control of a vast overseas empire. The cost to acquire this empire was enormous. In four colonial wars with France over 70 years, the public debt in Britain reached nearly £140,000,000, a staggering amount of money at the time and many times the annual revenue of the kingdom. Adding to this burden was the peacetime cost to maintain 6,000 regular troops in the colonies after 1763. King George III and his ministers attempted to levy new taxes in Great Britain, but these were met with strong opposition and so were quickly dropped. Money had to come from somewhere, so the British government turned to the American colonies.

For the most part, the colonies prospered during the French and Indian War (although the postwar economy went into decline). Britain's armies and fleets needed supplies of all kinds, and colonial merchants in places like New York, Philadelphia, and Boston were glad to provide the goods and services required to maintain Britain's military and naval operations during the war. While thousands of colonial "provincial" troops fought the French alongside Britain's regulars, the economic cost of the war was carried almost entirely by Great Britain. By the time the war ended in 1763, taxes in England were about 26 shillings per person and only about 1 shilling per person in the American colonies.

The desperate need for money led to a number of new colonial policies in the mid-1760s — mainly tax and trade laws that would anger many colonists. The resulting 12 year tug-of-war among King, Parliament and the American colonies grew ever more contentious and violent. Although there were supporters in Parliament of the American position, the arguments ended with the outbreak of the American Revolution in April, 1775. RT

The Great Lakes Seaway Trail

In a letter home to France early in 1758, the Marquis de Montcalm outlined his expectations for a possible eventual peace settlement with Britain. Such an agreement, he wrote, should include a British renunciation of claims to Lake Ontario, Lake Erie, and the Ohio Valley, and should restore French control in Acadia, which France had ceded to Britain in the 1713 Peace of Utrecht. In other words, French goals were relatively modest. With the British outnumbering the French in North America in 1754 approximately 27 to 1 (1,500,000 to 55,000), France could hardly expect more. Other than the restoration of Acadia, then, whose inhabitants were already predominantly French, the terms as envisioned by Montcalm would pretty much return North America to its pre-war status quo, keeping in check the territorial ambitions of the British and confining their settlements to the narrow strip along the Atlantic coast bounded on the west by the Appalachian Mountain chain.

At the core of this strategy of containment lay French mastery of the St. Lawrence River and the Great Lakes, the keystone of the main supply and communication route for a continuously fortified perimeter extending to the Gulf Coast. French control of this section of waterway would also enable trading to continue with tribes of the *pays d'en haut* and in itself be an effective and clearly defined barrier against incursions of the British. The 518 miles of today's Seaway Trail in New York and Pennsylvania parallel this waterway — the St. Lawrence River, Lake Ontario, Niagara River, and Lake Erie — that constituted the cornerstone to the French grand strategy.

Providing access to key 18th-century sites, the Seaway Trail brings alive the French and Indian War for the 21st-century traveler, and it does so in a uniquely satisfying fashion. At the western terminus of the Trail, the visitor finds the site marking the earliest face-to-face confrontation of the war at Fort Le Boeuf, where Washington's failed diplomatic mission set the stage for the conflict to follow. Proceeding along the Seaway Trail, the traveler eventually arrives at its eastern terminus, Fort Lévis, the focal point of the Battle of the Thousand Islands, and itself the final armed conflict leading to the capitulation of Montréal. Between those two chronological and material extremes lie Forts Presque Île (Isle), Niagara, Ontario, and Présentation, all testimony to the strategic importance of the waterway.

Fort de la Presque Île (Isle) now Erie, Pennsylvania, was the first of a series of forts constructed by the French in their attempt to establish a link between Lake Erie and the head of the Ohio River, a link designed to cut the British off from the Ohio Country while at the same time decrease travel time for the French to the Mississippi River. Fort Niagara's vantage overlooking the mouth of the Niagara River where it entered Lake Ontario allowed it to completely control traffic between Lake Ontario and Lake Erie. Fort Ontario's destruction by the French in 1756 eliminated all English presence on Lake Ontario, and Fort La Présentation's location on the St. Lawrence made it an invaluable source for funneling construction materials, trading goods, and provisions into the Ohio Country and the Great Lakes regions.

Britain's 1758 seizure of Fort Frontenac and her 1759 capture of Fort Niagara and refitting of Fort Ontario were thus the death knell of New France. With the loss to the English of this critical water link between Montreal and the Gulf Coast, the entire French enterprise in North America would come crashing down the following year.

The Seaway Trail

The Seaway Trail has been selected an America's Byway by the U. S. Federal Highway Administration, one of a select group of routes meeting elevated standards for scenic, natural, historic, cultural, archaeological and recreational values. The sites included in this guidebook have been selected for their relevance to the French and Indian War, but much more awaits the traveler of these roads. Those interested in military history will find collections relating to the Revolutionary War, the War of 1812, and on into 20th-century conflicts. Paralleling some of the finest natural water routes in the Northeast, Seaway Trail visitors can enjoy a wide range of educational, recreational and cultural activities, and can view wildlife, lighthouses, and unparalleled waterscapes, including Niagara Falls and the Thousand Islands. There truly is something for everybody. For more information, visit the Great Lakes Seaway Trail Discovery Center in Sackets Harbor, NY, an historic limestone building housing interactive exhibits on the War of 1812, lighthouses, historical personages, agriculture, recreation, and more, or contact Seaway Trail, Inc. through the contact information listed at the end of this guide. ■ SB

Look for a series of 20 interpretive signs along the Seaway Trail in New York and Pennsylvania.

The landscape of the Thousand Islands region of the St. Lawrence River on the U.S.-Canada border is little changed from the 1750s, despite a thriving tourism industry and modern highways. Photo courtesy Thousand Islands International Tourism Council.

Fort Le Boeuf

December 11, 1753. Early-winter snow was falling at Fort La Rivière aux Boeufs when a small travel-weary party of Virginians and Indians arrived at dusk carrying a message from the governor of Virginia, Robert Dinwiddie. Led by a 21-year-old, untested, headstrong young major named George Washington, the group included the experienced woodsman Christopher Gist (who at one point during the trip rescued Washington from the icy waters of the Allegheny), a translator (Washington spoke no French), and four Indians, among whom was the "Half-King" Tanaghrisson. They were entertained for five days while the French commandant, Captain Jacques Legardeur de Saint-Pierre, composed a reply. The 52-year-old Legardeur, described by Washington as "an elderly gentleman" and a veteran

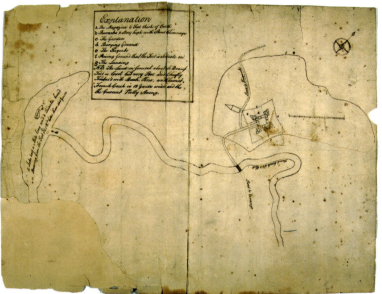

"Fort Le Boeuf by Thomas Hutchins." Hutchins (1730–1789) was a military engineer, map maker, geographer and surveyor, and was appointed "Geographer of the United States" in 1781. Courtesy Thomas Hutchins Papers, The Historical Society of Pennsylvania (HSP).

of posts throughout the French wilderness in North America, must have been somewhat bemused by the inexperienced Washington.

The construction of Fort Le Bouef had been completed that fall, the second in a chain of four forts intended to connect Lake Erie to the Ohio River. Illness and the difficulties of transporting supplies had delayed its completion, thereby postponing construction of the remaining two forts. Situated on French Creek at the end of a fifteen-mile portage from Fort Presque Île, the plan had been for a road to be built from Fort Presque Île on Lake Erie to Fort Le Boeuf, where goods could be transferred to bateaux to be floated down French Creek to Fort Machault at Venango where French Creek joined the Allegheny River, and then down the Allegheny to Fort Duquesne at the Forks of the Ohio. From there the Ohio would provide easy access to the Mississippi and French settlements in Louisiana.

In response to Governor Dinwiddie's claim that the French were encroaching on British soil and should leave, Captain Legardeur replied that, although French rights to the territory were "incontestable," the decision was not his to make, and that he would forward Dinwiddie's demands to the Marquis Duquesne, Governor of New France, for his consideration. Until he received directives to the contrary, however, he would continue to fulfill his orders to occupy his current position. Washington returned to Williamsburg carrying Legardeur's refusal, thus setting the stage for the armed hostilities which would begin the following spring.

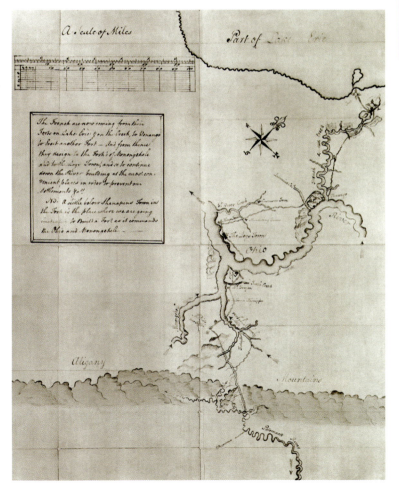

George Washington's map accompanying his "Journal to the Ohio," 1753–1754. Facsimile from Massachusetts Historical Society Collections, vol. 61. courtesy Wikimedia Commons.

A late 19th-century postcard depicting Fort Le Boeuf. Courtesy Donna Bluemink, usgwarchives.net.

Fort Le Boeuf would play a significant role throughout the war in forwarding men and materials into the Ohio Country, none more so than when Fort Duquesne was threatened by General Braddock's approach in 1755. The completion of Fort Machault in 1756, deeper in Indian country, took some of the pressure off Fort Le Boeuf, but it continued to play its part until the fall of Forts Duquesne in November, 1758, and Niagara the following July, made its position untenable. At that time the French abandoned the fort and burned it to the ground.

The strategic significance of Fort Le Boeuf's location, however, was not lost upon those who followed. Three countries were to occupy a fort on this site, of whom the French were only the first. After the fort burned in 1759, it was rebuilt by the English in 1760, only to be destroyed again during Pontiac's Rebellion in 1763 when the British garrison was forced to retreat to the more substantial Fort Pitt (the former Fort Duquesne). Thirty years later, in 1794, yet another conflict with Indians would necessitate its reconstruction by the Americans. ■ SB

Queen Aliquippa

Aliquippa, or "Queen" Aliquippa as the British called her, was a well-respected Seneca leader of a somewhat indeterminate age at the time of the French & Indian War. Not much is known about her, but what IS known is that she, unlike many other Senecas, provided unwavering support to the British, even to the point of joining Washington's forces in the ill-conceived defense of Fort Necessity.

Washington's first contact with her had come several months earlier, on his return from Fort Le Boeuf. Knowing how important her approval was to British/Seneca relations, and learning that she was upset, feeling that he had shown disrespect by not visiting her on his outbound trip, he made a 3-mile detour on his return, bringing her gifts of a matchcoat and a bottle of rum. SB

"I could get no certain account of the Number of Men here: But according to the best Judgment I could form, there are an Hundred exclusive of Officers, of which there are many. I also gave Orders to the People who were with me, to take an exact Account of the Canoes which were hauled up to convey their Forces down in the Spring. This they did, and told of 50 Birch Bark, and 170 of Pine; besides many others which were blocked-out, in Readiness to make."

From George Washington's observations regarding Fort Le Boeuf, December 13, 1753

● VISITING FORT LE BOEUF
Fort Le Boeuf Historical Society
Fort Le Boeuf Museum
31 High Street, Waterford PA
814-796-6030 (Historical Society)
814-732-2575 (Museum)
http://fortleboeuf.edinboro.edu/museum.html

- Saturdays and Sundays during the academic year, Noon – 4 p.m. or by appointment.
- Admission to the buildings is free.

Fort Tour Systems, Inc.
817-377-3678

Fortification during the French & Indian War

When artillery became powerful enough to smash medieval castle walls in the 15th century, European military engineers responded by designing forts with thick earthen walls. Partially hidden behind wide ditches and surrounding earthworks, these forts were much more resistant to the battering of massed cannon. They generally shared several key features — projecting bastions that flanked the connecting curtain walls, wide ramparts and parapets pierced for defending cannon and either a wet or dry ditch. Military engineers like the preeminent Frenchman Sébastien Le Prestre, Marquis de Vauban (1633–1707) or the Dutchman Baron van Coehoorn (1641–1704) devised increasingly elaborate "systems" of fortifications, designed to make it ever more difficult for a besieging force to overwhelm the defenders.

Experienced soldiers and engineers brought these concepts to North America, where fortifications were generally much simpler. For defense against Indians, a stout building or blockhouse surrounded by a palisade of logs was sufficient. Most of the frontier forts were just larger versions of this idea, but over time many began to show a more complex form, with bastions, fortified gates, and supporting outworks.

A few forts in North American, however, were built on a scale more typical of Europe, most notably Louisbourg on Cape Breton Island, Fort St. Frédéric on Lake Champlain, and Fort Carillon (Ticonderoga). These French forts all had well-engineered designs using stone in construction, and capable of withstanding all but the most determined siege. British forts like William Henry and Edward were built mainly of wood — walls were erected using cribs of heavy timbers filled with earth and rubble to give some protection from heavy cannon. Crown Point, begun toward the end of the French and Indian War and built of stone and wood, was the largest and most powerful British fortress. With the defeat of France, it became a fort without a purpose and by 1775 was largely a ruin.

Field fortifications — hastily dug trenches, log breastworks and obstacles such as *abatis* (a thicket of interwoven treetops and sharpened branches facing the enemy) — were common. The French lines at Carillon in 1758 are a good example of the effectiveness of these defenses.

As Vauban himself stated, no fortress could ultimately withstand the assault of a determined and patient besieger. Virtually all of the forts built by the French in North America were either taken by siege, assault or abandoned in the face of powerful British forces. RT

Fort de la Presque Île (Isle)

When Marquis Duquesne arrived in Montréal in 1752 as the Governor General for New France, he immediately began to implement plans for occupying the Ohio Valley. In the spring of 1753, work began on a series of four forts to provide a link between Lake Erie and the Ohio River. The first of those forts, located on the mainland near a peninsula, was Fort Presque Île, taking its name from the French word for peninsula, which meant "almost an island." Fort Presque Île (now Erie, Pennsylvania) and the second fort in the chain, Fort Le Boeuf, were situated to protect the ends of the Presque Île portage, a 15-mile carry from Lake Erie to French Creek. The portage, marking the highest altitude on the water route that extended from Montréal to New Orleans, placed the two forts on opposite sides of the divide. A canoe put in the water at Fort Le Boeuf would travel with the current all the way to the Gulf of Mexico. A canoe put in the water at Fort Presque Île would travel with the current all the way to the Gulf of St. Lawrence.

In contrast to Fort Le Boeuf, Fort Presque Île was constructed of squared chestnut logs with horizontal rather than vertical timbers. Covering an area one hundred twenty feet square, Fort Presque Île had triangular bastions at the corners, walls measuring twelve to fifteen feet high, and a complement of twelve guns. Captain Paul Marin, the commander of the French expedition charged with the construction of the forts, arrived at Presque Île on June 3, 1753. As soon as the French had occupied this first fort on the shore of Lake Erie, work crews immediately began to open the portage to French Creek. On August 3, Captain Marin notified Governor Duquesne that the fort had been completed, that a storehouse had been constructed at the midpoint of the portage, and that they were making good progress on the second fort.

Fort de la Presque Île, c. 1755, illustration by Robert McNamara, The Art of Wilderness/Seaway Trail, Inc..

The portage road did not hold up particularly well during the first winter. A July 15, 1754, letter from Captain Michel-Jean-Hugues Péan, an officer at Presque Île better known for his profiteering than for his dedication to the cause of New France, read: "I am going to have the entire three leagues of bad road in this portage paved with wood. I do not believe it possible to do it otherwise without always having to do it over again. That will be a lengthy piece of work but it will be durable." Later travelers commented on the durability of the corduroy road.

When Fort Niagara fell to the British in 1759, effectively closing off access to the Ohio country,

Interpretive signs tell the story of the three forts that were built in the area of Fort de la Presque Île (Isle).

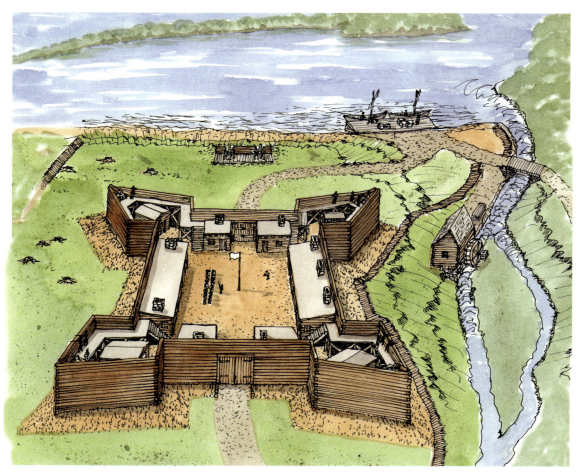

Fort Presque Île lost its usefulness and was burned and abandoned. Rebuilt by the British in 1760, it was one of the first victims of Pontiac's Rebellion, falling to a mixed force of Senecas, Chippewas, Ottawas, Wyandots, and Hurons in June, 1763. ■ SB

● VISITING FORT DE LA PRESQUE ÎLE (ISLE)

The "old French fort" was located between Front Street and Second Street, on the northeast side of Parade Street in Erie, PA
- There is a historic marker near the site of the forts, overlooking Lake Erie. The replica blockhouse is located at Second and Ash Streets, Erie, PA

The replica Wayne blockhouse at the Soldiers & Sailors Home, built in 1880, photo courtesy Erie County Historical Society.

Mad Anthony's body and bones

In 1796, General "Mad Anthony" Wayne was traveling home from a successful campaign against Indians in the Great Lakes area when he fell ill and died while passing through Presque Isle. There he was buried. In 1808, his children decided to move his remains to Radnor, Pennsylvania, for reburial in his home town. Lacking room in his carriage for a coffin, Isaac Wayne had his father's corpse boiled until the flesh dropped off. The bones were placed in a trunk and taken to Radnor where internment took place on July 4, 1809. The remaining flesh was reburied by the north blockhouse at the American Fort Presque Isle, thus creating two distinct burial sites for "Mad Anthony" Wayne, one for his bones and one for his flesh, almost 400 miles apart. In 1880 the Commonwealth of Pennsylvania built a replica blockhouse as a memorial to General Wayne. SB

The art of siege warfare during the French & Indian War

Since ancient times, the skills of the military engineer — in attack or defense — have always been highly valued. By the 18th century, siege warfare in Europe had evolved into a well-understood and universal set of procedures. While a fort might be captured suddenly by a *coup-de-main* or be delivered through treachery, forts in areas of active military operations were usually captured by siege.

The besieging force would arrive before the fortress and demand surrender. If the garrison refused, the besiegers would "open their trenches," establishing protective earthworks against a relieving force, building secure positions for heavy artillery and digging a first line of entrenchments from which to begin the advance upon a chosen section of the fort — the "first parallel."

From here, several zig-zag trenches were dug toward the fort — the angles of the zig-zag minimized casualties if the defenders fired directly into the trenches as soldiers worked with pick and shovel. The head of the advancing trench was called the "sap," protected by gabions, large earth-filled cylindrical wicker baskets. Gabions were also used to quickly build protective earthworks. At a closer distance to the fort, a second parallel would be dug and new, more effective positions for the heavy siege cannon would be erected.

The heavy cannon of the besiegers fired constantly at the fort, slowly battering down a section of the thick walls. The rubble from this bombardment also began to fill in the ditches. Large or elaborate forts often had additional protective works outside the main walls and bastions — redoubts, redans, ravelins, demilunes, or tenailles, each with a specialized defensive role — through which the besiegers had to force a way. Few forts in North America had such expensive extras.

A third and usually final parallel was dug very close to the fort. At this stage in a siege, unless a relieving force was near by, the fort and garrison were in imminent danger of capture. The heavy cannon by this time had made a breach — an opening though which the besiegers could storm the fort. The commander of the garrison would be summoned to surrender, and most did, preferring the "honors of war" offered by a gracious enemy to the hazards — and horrors — of a full-scale assault.

Of course the defenders did what they could to disrupt the progress of the siege. Sometimes a night attack or "sortie" on enemy positions would halt progress for a time, and disease and short supplies could affect both besieger and besieged. But given time, determination and adequate forces, no fortress — no matter how strong or well-supplied — could hold out indefinitely. The rude wooden forts of North America had little chance to stand up to determined besiegers well-supplied with artillery. RT

1. Soldiers (called sappers in English or *sapeurs* in French) digging at the head of the sap. Gabions are shown in green — the "head" of the sap is protected by a wheeled mantlet. **2.** A gabion. **3.** Cross-section of an earthen rampart. **4.** Cross-section of an emplacement for heavy siege cannon, with wooden platform for support.

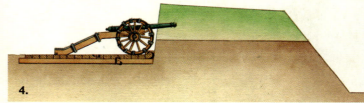

Illustrations come from a manuscript copy of Vauban's *Traite de Sieges de L'Attaque et Defense des Places*, 1714, courtesy Fort Ticonderoga Museum.

Old Fort Niagara

Strategically, Fort Niagara was at the epicenter of the storm that was the French & Indian War, a vital link in New France's effort to maintain the integrity of its lines of communication between Montréal, the Mississippi River and Louisiana. Situated on an elevated headland overlooking the entrance to the Niagara River from Lake Ontario, Fort Niagara not only controlled access to the portage around Niagara Falls that was the main conduit to the Great Lakes, but it served as a staging area for raids into the Ohio Country from Lake Erie.

The British were aware from the beginning of hostilities in 1754 that capturing Fort Niagara would effectively cut off communication and supplies to New France's western outposts. Events would dictate a lengthy incubation period, but the neutralization of Niagara would continue to be an essential objective in Britain's overall strategy of winning the war.

The first French installation to appear at the site had been Fort Conti in 1679, erected by La Salle as a base of operations while he built a sailing vessel to be used on the Great Lakes. This fort stood for less than a year before it accidentally burned and was abandoned. Concern over Iroquois aggression and British interest in the area prompted a second attempt in 1687. Fort Denonville, too, failed to become established. Harassed by the local Seneca population and decimated by uncompromising winter conditions, only 12 of the 100-man garrison survived the first winter, and the fort was quickly abandoned.

Above, the "castle" as seen today at Fort Niagara, courtesy Old Fort Niagara. At left: Plan of Fort Niagara, 1796, by George Henri Victor Collot, from "A Journey in North America…," The United States took over control of Fort Niagara from the British in 1796. Courtesy Cartography Associates, The David Rumsey Collection.

Overview of the siege of Fort Niagara, July 1759. The British trenches, saps and heavy artillery positions are seen at right, advancing toward the outworks protecting the ramparts of the fort, with their camps at far right. The strength and commanding position of Fort Niagara is clearly shown in this illustration by Robert McNamara, The Art of Wilderness/Seaway Trail, Inc..

Fort Niagara was captured by the British in December, 1813, during the War of 1812.

It was not until 1726 that the *Maison à Machicoulis*, what in the 19th century became known as the "French Castle", and the heart of Fort Niagara was constructed. Assuring the Iroquois that they were only building a trading post, the French erected a stone edifice equipped to survive any Indian attack. A "machicolated" structure, the source of its name, had medieval-style openings from which to fire on attackers.

During the 1750s, when the threat of a British assault became a major concern, Fort Niagara's defenses were greatly expanded. Between 1755 and 1757, Niagara was transformed into a much larger fortress of essentially European configurations under the direction of Captain Pierre Pouchot. The old wooden stockade was replaced by solid earthwork defenses, and the number of supporting structures — barracks, hospital, masonry powder magazine, forge, stable, bakehouse, and church — was increased many times over.

Those efforts came to naught in 1759 when a British force under General John Prideaux laid siege to the fort for 19 days. Niagara's commanding officer, Captain Pouchot, whose normally reliable source of intelligence, the Senecas, had transferred their loyalty to the British, was not aware of an impending attack and had sent the majority of his soldiers to engage in operations in the Ohio Country. Left with only 500 defenders against an attacking force of 3,500, his only hope was the timely return of his garrison in response to a plea for assistance. Those men never made it back, being intercepted and defeated by a detachment sent by Sir William Johnson a few miles upriver from the fort at a spot known as *La Belle Famille*. Johnson had assumed command after General Prideaux stepped in front of one of his own mortars during the siege. Pouchot surrendered to Johnson on July 25, and New France's link to her western outposts was severed. ■ SB

● VISITING OLD FORT NIAGARA
2 Scott Ave, P.O. Box 169, Youngstown, NY 14174
716-745-7611   www.oldfortniagara.org
http://nysparks.state.ny.us/sites
- Old Fort Niagara is open all year. Check the website for seasonal hours, admission prices, and group tour information.
- Closed January 1, U.S. Thanksgiving, December 25.

Annual living history events at Old Fort Niagara interpret the French and Indian War (above), American Revolution, and the War of 1812.

Weapons of war in the 1750s

The soldiers of the French and Indian War were all armed and equipped in a similar manner. The British .75 caliber Long Land musket and the .69 caliber French Model 1728 musket were the principal firearms. Similar in capability, both were flintlock smoothbores reasonably effective at 100 yards, firing a destructive soft lead ball. Each army had its own drill — a series of maneuvers and steps to enable the controlled movement of massed troops and operation of weapons. A well-trained soldier could load and fire his musket two to three times per minute. Ammunition consisted of a paper cartridge containing gunpowder and a ball. Soldiers carried anywhere from 18 to as many as 60 rounds. These muskets mounted a bayonet — a fearsome and effective weapon in the hands of determined troops. Other small arms included swords for officers and cavalrymen, pole arms, pistols, axes and tomahawks.

There were several types of cannon used during the French and Indian War. The most common were field guns, mounted on wheeled wooden carriages, firing iron cannon balls from 3 to 12 pounds in weight and deadly grapeshot or canister rounds. Howitzers, short, wide-mouthed cannon firing exploding shells were also used in the field. For siege work, heavy cannon firing 24-pound balls were used to batter down fortifications, and mortars lobbed exploding shells in a high arc into the interior of a fort or town. These specialized heavy guns were almost never used in battle since they were difficult to transport and required large supplies of ammunition. RT

The British .75 caliber Long Land musket. Historical Image Bank.

The .69 caliber French Model 1728 musket. Historical Image Bank.

A typical "6-pounder" cannon, mounted on a wheeled field carriage, with examples of tools and ammunition.

Mortars were short-barrelled artillery pieces that came in many sizes — all fired an explosive projectile in a high arc to clear walls or obstacles.

Illustrations by Robert McNamara, The Art of Wilderness/Seaway Trail, Inc..

Fort Ontario SHS (Oswego)

When General William Shirley arrived at Fort Oswego in 1755 to oversee preparations for launching an attack on Fort Niagara, he found the fort in a state of hopeless disrepair. Realizing that the facility was totally inadequate as a base of supplies for the Niagara campaign, he suspended plans for a 1755 attack, preferring to strengthen the Oswego site for a 1756 operation instead.

England's only toehold on Lake Ontario, Fort Oswego had been poorly designed when it was first built in 1727. Expanded from a seasonal trading post on the west side of the river, the initial stone construction was exposed to the threat of cannon fire from high ground overlooking the fort. Shirley ordered construction in the fall of 1755 to begin on two additional facilities, a more substantial eight-pointed stockade to be known as Fort Ontario on the east bank, and a smaller structure on a bluff to the west, Fort George (derisively nicknamed "Fort Rascal" by the men assigned to defend it).

With the fort's supply line from Albany having been disrupted by French and Indian attacks, the fort was still undermanned and unprepared when a force of 4,000 men with eighty cannon under the command of the Marquis de Montcalm attacked on August 10, 1756. Fort Ontario, under the threat of guns at point blank range, was quickly abandoned, and the British defenders sought shelter in the equally inadequate Fort Oswego. When the British commanding officer, Lieutenant Colonel James Mercer, was beheaded by a cannon ball, his dispirited replacement, Lieutenant Colonel John Littlehales, asked for terms within the hour. Montcalm, disdainful of such a poorly mounted defense, refused to grant the British the honors of war and took the entire garrison prisoner, guaranteeing them only safe passage to Montréal. He soon learned that he had promised more than he could deliver. In an incident ominously anticipating events the following year at Fort William Henry, Montcalm's Indian contingent killed between 30 and 40 patients in the garrison hospital and took dozens of prisoners before heading back to their villages. Despite his inability to control his Indian allies, however, and confident that any threat from the British on Lake Ontario had been eliminated, Montcalm destroyed the fortifications at Oswego and returned to Montréal.

A somewhat fanciful engraving of the harbor and defenses of Oswego from *The London Magazine*, 1760. Courtesy Randy Patten.

"A View of Fort Oswego on the Shore Lake Ontario," by T. Clarke, 1799. Courtesy Randy Patten.

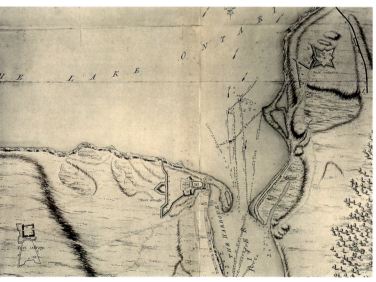
A sketch of the Oswego defenses in 1756, with Fort Ontario at upper right, Fort George at center, and Fort Oswego at left. The harbor channels are clearly marked with depth notations. Courtesy Randy Patten.

● **VISITING FORT ONTARIO**
1 East 4th St., Oswego, NY 13126
315-343-4711. or 315-343-1430
www.fortontario.com
nysparks.state.ny.us/sites

- Fort Ontario is open mid-May through mid-October. Check the website for seasonal hours, admission prices and group tour information.

Fort Ontario lay in ruins for the next three years. By 1759 circumstances had changed. With Great Britain gaining the upper hand, plans for a renewed assault on Fort Niagara became plausible. General Prideaux, in his passage to Niagara, left a force of 1,000 men to rebuild Fort Ontario. Fighting off an attack by the French when their attackers relinquished the element of surprise by stopping to pray within full view of the fort, the British erected a new pentagonal, earthen-work structure, the basic foundation for what remains today. With Fort Frontenac having capitulated in 1758, and Fort Niagara in 1759, the British took control of Lake Ontario. Fort Ontario then became, in 1760, the base of operations when General Amherst left with a force of more than 10,000 men as part of the final assault on what remained of New France on the St. Lawrence River. ■ SB

Visitors to Fort Ontario State Historic Site today will see the star-shaped fort restored to its 1868–1872 appearance. By then this type of fort had become obsolete. Courtesy Fort Ontario SHS.

Reenactors portraying French troops defend a position protected by a makeshift abatis at a living history event at Fort Ontario. Courtesy Fort Ontario SHS.

The Marquis de Montcalm

Louis-Joseph de Montcalm, Marquis de Montcalm (1712–1759) commanded French forces in North America during most of the French and Indian War. He served in the War of the Polish Succession (1733–1738) and the War of Austrian Succession (1740–1748), becoming a colonel in 1743 and a general in 1748. He was sent to Québec in 1756 to replace Baron de Dieskau who had been taken prisoner at the Battle of Lake George in 1755. Montcalm took Fort Oswego in 1756 and successfully besieged Fort William Henry in 1757. Montcalm's army was victorious again at Fort Carillon in 1758, but French strategy demanded the defense of Québec the next year, even if that meant abandoning the frontier posts of Fort St. Frédéric and Carillon. He was mortally wounded at the Battle of Québec on September 13, 1759, dying the next day. His army was defeated and the British captured this important city, key to the defense of Canada. RT

Pastel portrait courtesy Fort Ticonderoga Museum.

Fort de La Présentation

More a commercial outpost than a military installation, Fort de La Présentation was ideally situated to relay supplies to French forts in the interior. Located on a small peninsula about 60 miles downstream from Lake Ontario at the mouth of the Oswegatchie River where it empties into the St. Lawrence, the small garrison at Fort de La Présentation utilized its relatively easy access to Lake Ontario and Fort Niagara to funnel supplies through Niagara and the Falls portage to Lake Erie and the Ohio Country. Building materials, food, livestock, and locally produced items such as snowshoes, moccasins, and clothing all made their way into frontier posts from the fort.

The fort was roughly 150 feet square, with a blockhouse in each corner, the whole connected with a wooden stockade to shelter its inhabitants. A Sulpician priest, Abbé François Picquet, had constructed the fort in 1749 as a mission to Native Americans, intent on converting nearby Iroquois not only to Catholicism, but to French efforts to keep the encroaching British at bay. Indians looking to settle near the fort had to agree to two conditions — they had to forswear the use of alcohol, and they had to honor the Christian commitment to monogamy.

Quite successful in his proselytizing, by the mid-1750s Father Picquet had drawn about 3,000 Onondagas, Oneidas, Senecas, and Cayugas into the surrounding area. Such a ready source of fighters could not be ignored. Warriors drawn from what became known as the Oswegatchie population took part in raids on English settlements in the Mohawk Valley, the Champlain Valley, and on Lake Ontario, often accompanied by Father Picquet. An uncommonly active cleric, his presence was noted in 1755 at Braddock's defeat, in 1756 at the destruction of Forts Bull (near Rome, New York) and Oswego, in 1757 at Fort William Henry, and in 1758 at Fort Carillon. He has sometimes been blamed for not controlling the Indians under his charge and for

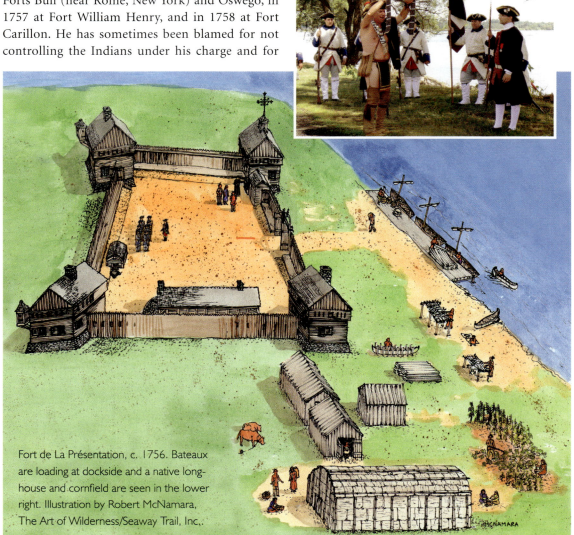

French and Indian reenactors recreate a ceremonial exchange of gifts in friendship on the banks of the St. Lawrence River during a Fort de La Présentation annual Founder's Day living history event. Photo courtesy Fort de La Présentation Association.

The original cornerstone of Fort de La Présentation, erected in 1749 by Abbé Francois Picquet, begun as a mission to the Indians. Courtesy Fort de La Présentation Association.

Fort de La Présentation, c. 1756. Bateaux are loading at dockside and a native longhouse and cornfield are seen in the lower right. Illustration by Robert McNamara, The Art of Wilderness/Seaway Trail, Inc.

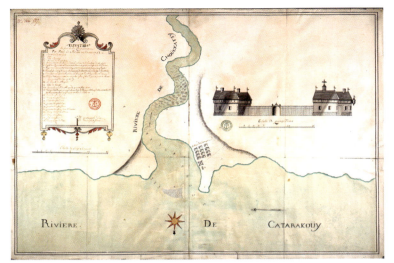

A 1752 French map clearly shows the fort and Oswegatchie settlement and also gives a measured elevation drawing of the fort, reference for the eventual construction of a replica on the site. Courtesy Library and Archives of Canada.

permitting the carnage that took place after the surrender of Fort William Henry as the paroled British forces left the fort heading for Fort Edward.

As the land under control of the French shrank in 1758 and 1759, as the forts at Louisbourg, Frontenac, Duquesne, Carillon and Niagara fell in succession, and as Montcalm pulled back from the Champlain Valley to concentrate his forces in the St. Lawrence Valley, it became clear that Fort de La Présentation, now on the western periphery of French defenses, provided inadequate fortifications to withstand a sustained assault. In 1759 it was abandoned over Father Picquet's objections in favor of construction of a new fort, Fort Lévis, on Île Royale (now Chimney Island) a little further downstream.

During the Battle of the Thousand Islands in 1760, an important naval engagement took place off the peninsular location of Fort de la Présentation. Five row galleys under the command of Colonel George Williamson, each mounted with a single gun — one a howitzer and the others 12-pounders — utilized their greater mobility to defeat the French corvette *l'Outaouaise* in a bloody battle lasting more than three hours. The captured crew was taken and confined in the abandoned Fort de la Présentation. The *l'Outaouaise*, repaired and renamed the HMS *Williamson*, then took part in the ensuing siege of Fort Lévis.

After the fall of New France, the British occupied Fort de La Présentation, renaming it Fort Oswegatchie. Under the Jay Treaty implemented in 1796, Fort Oswegatchie was transferred to the Americans and given an anglicized version of its original name, Fort Presentation. ■ SB

● VISITING FORT DE LA PRÉSENTATION
Fort La Présentation Association

P. O. Box 1749, Ogdensburg, New York 13669   www.fortlapresentation.net
Fort de la Présentation is located at Lighthouse Point in Ogdensburg, New York.

Compagnies franches de la marine

The Navy Department administered overseas French colonies and garrisoned them with *troupes de la marine*, first raised in 1683. By 1757 this force consisted of 40 companies based in New France. These units — they formed the garrison of Canada — were known as the *compagnies franches de la marine* (Independent Companies of the Navy). Generally well-uniformed and equipped, on campaign they may have adopted more informal dress. The figure here is shown without his tricorne hat and regulation unbleached wool uniform coat, and wears Indian-style leggings and moccasins. They were nonetheless experienced fighters, often a match for the Indians in hit-and-run warfare and fought in all the campaigns of the French & Indian War. The soldiers were recruited in France, and were expected to remain in New France when their service was complete. Clothing and arms were manufactured in France and sent to Canada for distribution. RT

Painting by Don Troiani, Historical Image Bank.

The site of Fort de La Présentation on Lighthouse Point in Ogdensburg, NY. Courtesy Fort de La Présentation Association.

Fort Lévis

Captain Pierre Pouchot, the same Captain Pouchot who had been forced to surrender Fort Niagara the year before after a long siege and in the face of insurmountable odds, must have had a sense of *déjà vu* in 1760. Captured and then released in a prisoner exchange, he now found himself placed in charge of hardly more than 300 men manning unfinished fortifications on a small island in the middle of a river down which an invading force of 11,000 men was approaching.

By the end of 1759, the territory controlled by New France had been reduced to the area immediately surrounding Montréal. British commander Jeffery Amherst planned a three-pronged attack in 1760. General James Murray would move up the St. Lawrence from Québec, General William Haviland would advance from the south through the Lake Champlain/Richelieu River corridor, and General Amherst himself would move down the St. Lawrence from Oswego. The three forces would converge on Montréal permitting no escape. Chevalier de Lévis, successor to Montcalm, knew that his only hope lay in disrupting the coordinated attack of the three armies. To accomplish that, he ordered the construction of a new fort on Île Royale (now Chimney Island), an island one hundred miles upstream from Montréal directly in the path of Amherst's army. Here, as commander of the new Fort Lévis, Pouchot was given the unenviable task of performing the impossible.

Originally intended to be constructed of stone and to house a garrison of 2,500 men supported by 200 cannon, Fort Lévis consisted of wooden and earth walls and an odd assortment of soldiers, seamen, and militia armed with only a

Low-lying Chimney Island, the site of Fort Lévis, was reduced to 6 acres in 1957 during the construction of the St. Lawrence Seaway. Photo courtesy Barbara O'Keefe.

Fort Lévis was named in honor of the Duc de Lévis, second in command to Montcalm and senior French officer after Montcalm's death in September 1759. Amherst's attacks on Fort Lévis lasted from August 16 through the 26, 1760. Illustration by Robert McNamara, The Art of Wilderness/Seaway Trail, Inc..

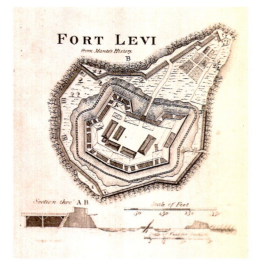

Notes written on the back of this print state that this is a plan of "Fort Levi" on Chimney Island — the English name of the island — called *Oraconenton* by the Indians and by the French *Île Royal* or *Oraqointon*. Courtesy Fort La Présentation Association.

few cannon. No help would be coming from the neighboring Catholic, pro-French Iroquois, all of whom had been convinced by emissaries of Amherst's Iroquois to at least stand aside, to remain neutral.

When British forces attacked in August 1760, Pouchot and his handful of men put up stiff resistance, disabling all three of Amherst's attacking ships and absorbing fire from British batteries overlooking the fort from the St. Lawrence shore and nearby islands. For five days, Fort Lévis withstood a pounding, including, on the final day, a barrage of hot shot — red hot cannon balls which set the fort's debris on fire. Numbers are somewhat contradictory, but at least 80 percent of the defenders were killed or wounded during the onslaught. Only after Pouchot had exhausted all his own ammunition and the fort had been reduced to a pile of rubble did he ask for terms, surrendering on August 26.

Unfortunately for the French, the heroic defense of Fort Lévis only served to delay the inevitable. Amherst's army now had an open path to Montréal, where the threat of attack by British forces coming from three directions forced Governor Vaudreuil to capitulate, effectively bringing an end to the French presence in North America.

Fort Lévis would be rebuilt by the British, rechristened Fort William Augustus, and serve as a supply source for British forces in North America through the American revolutionary period. ■ SB

● VISITING FORT LÉVIS
Chimney Island, the site of Fort Lévis, is currently not open to the public, but may be viewed from shore, from the bridge, or from the water. There are several websites that provide additional information.

The Battle of the Thousand Islands 16–24 August 1760

The Battle of the Thousand Islands was part siege and part naval engagement. Accounts of the battle list a varied assortment of naval vessels and watercraft. Armed vessels included row galleys, a brig, a schooner, and two snows (pronounced "snoo" or "snaw"). A brig is a two-masted, square-rigged vessel with a gaff-rigged "spanker" sail on the mainmast. A snow is a brig with a small auxiliary mast just aft of the mainmast to which the spanker is attached, separating the spanker from the mainmast and providing easier operation of the mainmast sails.

The French ships — the schooner *Iroquoise* and the brig *Outaouaise* — slipped into the St. Lawrence from Lake Ontario ahead of the two British snows, the *Mohawk* and the *Onondaga*. Heading downriver, the *Iroquoise* ran aground on a shoal and was pulled off, arriving at Fort Lévis badly damaged. Without time or manpower for repairs, she was beached, out of action, where she lay on her side, port guns buried in the sand and starboard guns pointing skyward. The *Outaouaise* took up a position as an advance guard for Fort Lévis, but was captured on August 17 after a two-hour battle with 5 British row galleys, each armed with a 12-pounder cannon in the bow. Meanwhile, the 2 British snows, having been lured by a French row galley, were floundering in the maze of the 1000 Islands, wasting several days finding their way out!

On the 23rd, having finally arrived off Fort Lévis, the two snows along with the *Williamson* (the *Outaouaise*, repaired, refitted, and renamed by the British) turned their combined 44 guns on the island, only to be driven off and disabled by the 5 guns of the fort. The *Onondaga* ran aground, where she was subjected to a brutal battering from the fort's guns, suffering heavy casualties and eventual destruction. The British shore batteries continued their barrage, however, until Fort Lévis was forced to surrender on August 25. SB

Thomas Davies, "A View of Fort La Galette [Fort de La Présentation], Indian Castle, and Taking a French Ship of War on the River St. Lawrence, by Four Boats of One Gun Each of the Royal Artillery Commanded by Captain Streachy," 1760. Courtesy National Gallery of Canada, Ottawa.

Revolutionary Byway

Flanked by the Adirondacks to the north and the Allegheny plateau to the south, the Mohawk River Valley slashes through the Appalachian Mountain chain, affording access to the Great Lakes and beyond. In the mid-eighteenth century, it was the only available natural water route into the interior North American continent for the British colonists.

The Dutch had been the first Europeans to venture into the valley, when, in 1634, Harmen van den Bogaert led a small party into Iroquois territory to discover the cause of a decrease in the fur trade. Even then, more than a hundred years before the start of the French and Indian War, the lines were drawn. Van den Bogaert discovered that the French had, in fact, been making overtures to the Iroquois, but that the Iroquois still would prefer to trade with the Dutch because of Iroquois hostility to the Indian companions of the French, the Hurons. Van den Bogaert's diplomacy would ensure that the river would function as a commercial artery for first Dutch, and then British, trappers and traders and their Iroquois allies.

Count de Frontenac, Governor General of Canada, did lead a raiding party up the Oswego River in 1696 against the Onondagas, but the French decided not to establish a foothold at the mouth of the river. European occupation of the site did not occur until 1722 when Albany fur traders established a trading post, an enterprise that was strengthened with stonework at the direction of New York Governor Burnet in 1727. The resulting installation, Fort Oswego, along with the friendship of the Iroquois through whose land the route lay, secured the Albany-Ontario passage for the British.

Overt hostility between France and Britain had produced isolated French and Indian raids in the Valley, notably the 1690 massacre at Schenectady, but it was not until the beginning of the French and Indian War in 1754 that both sides tried to seriously exploit both the strategic importance and the inherent vulnerabilities of the region. Because of the exposed positions of earlier settlements and trading posts, most pre-war sites had been protected either by stockades (Schenectady) or were individual homes constructed of stone and designed for defense (Fort Klock, Old Fort Johnson).

During the war, the British tried to reinforce key and vulnerable points along the route. They first tried to secure their toehold on Lake Ontario with the construction of Forts Ontario and George at the mouth of the Oswego River and to protect both ends of the Oneida Carry. Marquis de Montcalm's destruction of the forts at Oswego in 1756 and General Webb's panicked flight from the Valley, destroying all British defenses in the process, brought British fortunes in the region to a low point. The way now lay open for a French invasion force to penetrate to the core of the New York colony. With the shift of French forces to defend against Abercromby's 1758 campaign on Lake George and the fall of Forts Frontenac and Niagara on Lake Ontario, however, the threat in the Valley effectively disappeared. The British filled the vacuum with construction of new forts at Oswego (Fort Ontario) and the Oneida Carry (Forts Brewerton and Stanwix). These new efforts quickly proved their value. Amherst's 3-pronged thrust in 1760 utilized the Mohawk corridor to transport men and supplies to Fort Ontario, from where his army of 11,000 moved down the St. Lawrence to converge with the armies of General Murray and General Haviland in the final assault on Montréal.

Symbolic of the pronounced changes in the Valley brought about by the British triumph was Sir William Johnson's decision in 1762 to move from Fort Johnson to more refined quarters at Johnson Hall. More tumultuous disorder would lie in the future with the onset of the Revolution, but for now the Mohawk Valley reveled in an entirely new sense of security that would last until the American Revolution.

The Revolutionary Byway

The beautiful Mohawk Valley is unusual in its rich concentration of history and tradition. Not only does the river valley provide the only east-west water-level route through the Appalachian Mountain chain, but by the early 18th century it had become the nexus of interaction among four distinct cultures—Dutch, Palatine German, English, and Iroquois. It was a potent mix.

In 1997 eight counties east of Oneida Lake joined to create the Mohawk Valley Heritage Corridor, a partnership of public and private organizations that spearheaded the development of the Revolutionary Byway the full length of this historic water route. A trip along the Revolutionary Byway exposes the visitor to layers of history, from the pre-contact period of Iroquois control through the arrival of the Dutch, the late-17th-century raids on English-governed Dutch settlers by the French and their Canadian Indian allies, the arrival of the Palatine Germans in the early 18th century, the French and Indian War, the devastation caused by the Revolution, the construction of the Erie Canal, and on into the present. Sites and artifacts from every era have been preserved and are accessible to the 21st-century visitor on the Revolutionary Byway. This is time travel at its best. For contact information, refer to the resources section of this guidebook. ■ SB

The Mohawk River, now part of the NYS Barge Canal for much of its 140-mile length, still winds its way through countryside that in many ways is little changed from the 18th century. Photo by Bart M. Carrig, courtesy Mohawk Valley Heritage Corridor Commission.

Schenectady Stockade

In the bitter cold and darkness of a February night, shadowy figures slipped through the unguarded gate and spread silently throughout the settlement. When all were in place, a war whoop announced the onset of slaughter. Chaos ensued. Of the village's 130 inhabitants, 60 were killed and another 27 taken prisoner. The French and Indian raiding party, having accomplished its goal, now turned and headed home to Montréal.

The scene for this massacre was Schenectady, 1690, more than sixty years before the British and French armies and their respective Indian allies collided in the war for the continent that is called the French and Indian War. Schenectady, exposed on the edge of the wilderness twenty miles west of Albany, would endure countless more raids, none as immediately devastating, perhaps, but nonetheless cre-

This carefully-researched painting by Len Tantillo depicts Schenectady on the eve of the raid in 1690. Courtesy Schenectady County Historical Society.

ating an atmosphere of uncertainty and fear in their swiftness and deadliness. Raiders sought more than scalps and captives, symbols of their prowess in war. They sought to drive the English from the frontier, to maintain their control over inland North America.

What is noteworthy about this first raid, perhaps, more than its suddenness and ferocity, was the route taken by the raiding party. Having departed Montréal, they made their way quickly down the frozen Lake Champlain to the bend in the Hudson River marking the site of the future Fort Edward. From there, they descended the Hudson to the junction of the Mohawk, and then ascended the Mohawk to the stockaded village of Schenectady. Decades later, armies would move along

The site of the blockhouse at the "Queen's Fort" (completed in 1705) is the junction of Front, Green and North Ferry Streets in Schenectady. A statue was erected here in 1887, dedicated to "Lawrence the Indian." Lawrence was a Christian Mohawk who was a great friend to the early settlers and the most dogged of those who tracked the retreating French and Indians and their prisoners after the 1690 raid. During the French and Indian War the "Queen's Fort" was strengthened and the stockade area enlarged. Photo courtesy Randy Patten.

The Mabee Farm Historic Site

The oldest house still standing in the Mohawk Valley, the Mabee Farm Historic Site was originally settled by Daniel Janse Van Antwerpen in 1671, who established it as a fur-trading post to meet Native American traders before they reached Schenectady. In 1706, Van Antwerpen sold the western portion of his land to Jan Pieterse Mabee and the home remained in the Mabee family for 287 years. The original structures on the site include the stone farmhouse, brick slave quarters, and an early 19th-century tavern predating the Erie Canal (1825). A family cemetery has graves dating back to the 1700s. The 1760 Nilsen Dutch barn, an English-style barn, and several outbuildings replace the originals which burned down in the early 20th century. The Mabee Farm is owned by the Schenectady County Historical Society and hosts several living history (photo at right) and other public events each year.

Mabee Farm Historic Site, 1080 Main Street, Rotterdam Junction, NY 12150 518-887-5073 www.schist.org/mabee.

Schenectady c. 1763, from John Rocque, *A Set of Plans and Forts in America, Reduced from Actual Surveys*, London, Mary Ann Rocque, 1763. D is the "Stockade planted round the Town," B is the "Wooden fort," and C are "Block houses to defend the Stockades." Courtesy New York State Library.

the same routes followed by this early Canadian raiding party, the same waterways that would become the highways of war.

Schenectady's location on the Mohawk just west of Albany made it a natural staging area for that later conflict. Troops gathered and provisions were packed there before armies set out west through the Mohawk Valley for targets in the Lake Ontario theater. One of those targets was Fort Frontenac, located at the east end of Lake Ontario. Guarding the entrance to the St. Lawrence River, Fort Frontenac was a key element in the lucrative trade that the French enjoyed with Indians in the Great Lakes. Serving as a major warehouse, its capture would not only close off that trade and break the link between New France and its western allies, but would remove a major source of war materials for the French forts in the Ohio Valley.

In July, 1758, Lieutenant Colonel John Bradstreet used Schenectady's strategic location to set up his move on Frontenac. Gathering an army of 5,600 soldiers could hardly be done in secret, so disguising his army's objective was critical in maintaining the element of surprise. Knowing that the French would have eyes and ears in Schenectady, Bradstreet let it be widely known that his army's assignment was the reconstruction of the English fort at the Great Carrying Place, a goal that the French would not find immediately threatening. His duplicitous plan worked to perfection. French intelligence reported the British intention of rebuilding Fort Bull; once at the Great Carrying Place, Bradstreet moved quickly to Lake Ontario; and in August his army captured a lightly defended and completely surprised Fort Frontenac. ■ SB

● VISITING THE SCHENECTADY STOCKADE
Schenectady County Historical Society

- 32 Washington Avenue, Schenectady, New York 12305   518-374-0263   www.schist.org
- For more infomration about visiting the Stockade area and events go to www.historicstockade.com, www.schenectadyhistory.org and www.dmna.state.ny.us/forts/fortsQ_S/schenectadyStockade

Each year, the public enjoys the Walkabout (above), Waterfront Faire. and an annual Art Show. There are over 40 pre-Revolutionary War buildings in the Stockade area. Photo courtesy Schenectady County Historical Society.

Colonel John Bradstreet

Despite the fact that John Bradstreet (1714–1774) devised, choreographed, and achieved one of the most significant victories of the French and Indian War, his name has none of the recognition factor that accompanies those of Amherst, Wolfe, Johnson, Montcalm, Rogers, and Braddock. His stunning 1758 capture of Fort Frontenac was a turning point in the war, severing the French line of communications on the St. Lawrence, cutting off French forces in the Great Lakes region and the Ohio Valley from their source of men and materials, convincing New France's western Indian allies to withdraw their support, and triggering the drastic shrinkage of New France's formerly vast territorial claims.

As early as 1755, Bradstreet, recognizing the strategic importance of Frontenac's location at the juncture of the St. Lawrence River and Lake Ontario, had pressed for an attack. Permission was granted, but then began a series of crises and command decisions that prevented Bradstreet from carrying out his plan for three years. His talents, particularly in organizing and implementing critical bateaux transport, were needed elsewhere.

Finally, in the summer of 1758, Bradstreet, to keep his plans secret, let it be known in Schenectady that he was preparing to move up the Mohawk Valley to the Oneida Carry with a sizable force to rebuild a fort destroyed earlier by the French. Once there he kept right on going to Lake Ontario and Fort Frontenac, battering a surprised, unprepared, and undermanned garrison into hasty submission, a penetrating and crippling blow that undermined the entire territorial integrity of New France.

In 1759, Bradstreet was made Deputy Quartermaster-General, and was promoted to Major General in May, 1772. He died in New York City on September 25, 1774. SB

Old Fort Johnson

His name was *Warraghiyagey*. A Mohawk name given to one of their own, a remarkable man who just happened to be Irish. He seemed to be everywhere. He commanded the provincials at the Battle of Lake George; he mobilized the largest Native contingent ever to field with the British during the war in 1758; he was in charge when the British took Fort Niagara; and he shared in the final assault on the city of Montréal. He dressed in a loin cloth and adorned his body with paint, porcupine quills, and anklet deer bones which rattled when he danced. He ate ceremonial dog meat, and he was knighted by the King of England. His name was William Johnson.

Johnson was a man who slipped back and forth easily between two cultures. Having arrived in America in 1738 from Ireland as a twenty-one-year-old, sent by his family to manage his uncle's property in the Mohawk Valley, Johnson soon bought property of his own and began to engage in trade with neighboring Mohawks. The fair-mindedness and integrity he brought to the process attracted the Mohawks, who were accustomed to dealing with unscrupulous traders out to profit at the Indians' expense. Johnson in turn was attracted by the rich and expressive Iroquois culture. He learned the Mohawk tongue, took part in their rituals, and was adopted into their family and given the name Warraghiyagey, ("doer of great things" or "chief big business" or "he in charge of affairs").

Recognizing his value in conducting diplomacy with the Iroquois, New York Governor George Clinton, in 1744, appointed him to the first of

The buildings and grounds around Fort Johnson, from a sketch by William Johnson's nephew and deputy agent Colonel Guy Johnson, printed in the *Royal Magazine* in 1759. A, B, and C make up the fort itself, and the rest are supporting structures including barns, stables and an aqueduct (H) to provide water to the mill (G). The steep Mount Johnson is N and the Mohawk River is Q. Courtesy Randy Patten.

The great Cohoes Falls on the Mohawk River, near where the Mohawk River meets the Hudson, was a considerable obstacle as seen in this 1761 print. Waterborne cargo had to be unloaded and carried by portage around the falls before proceeding upstream or downstream. Courtesy Library of Congress.

Old Fort Johnson seen from the front. While the stone and wood needed to build the house were obtained locally, items such as hardware, window glass, marble, lead paint and even some specialized tools had to be imported from Europe. Photo courtesy Randy Patten.

Visitors can see the original loopholes made through the thick stone walls that allowed defenders to fire their muskets at attackers. Photo courtesy Old Fort Johnson.

his official posts in Indian affairs, which eventually led in 1755 to his appointment by General Edward Braddock as Superintendent of Northern Indian Affairs, a title he would carry for the remainder of his life.

By the mid-1740s, Johnson was living in a three-story stone house on his property north of the Mohawk River. As tensions increased with the onset of the third of the Anglo-French Wars, and in deference to his exposed position at the edge of the wilderness, Johnson fortified his home, which became known as Fort Johnson. It also became a central meeting ground for conferences with the Iroquois. One of the largest gatherings took place in 1755, in the months leading to Johnson's first large military exercise. Having been placed in charge of a proposed campaign against Fort St. Frédéric on Lake Champlain, Johnson appealed to his Mohawk brethren to play a role in support of the British. A council fire of the Iroquois League was lit on his property, attracting upwards of a thousand Indians. Of that thousand, only 300, perhaps, were warriors. The rest were women and children. The proceedings went on for several days, the Indians camping out on Johnson's property and enjoying the hospitality he knew was required. As he wrote to Governor DeLancy, "I am distressed where to get victuals for such numbers; they have destroyed every green thing upon my estate and destroyed all my meadows. But I must humor them at this critical juncture."

His efforts bore fruit. At the September encounter with Baron Dieskau's French troops which became known as the Battle of Lake George, Johnson's army included 200 Mohawk warriors, many who gave their lives, including the venerable Mohawk chief Theyanoguin, known to the British as "King Hendrick." ■ SB

● VISITING OLD FORT JOHNSON
Montgomery County Historical Society
Old Fort Johnson is located at the corner of Routes 5 and 67, Fort Johnson, NY 12070 518-843-0300
www.oldfortjohnson.org
- Open May 15 through October 15, Wednesday through Saturday 10:00 a.m. to 4:00 p.m. Sundays 1:00 p.m. to 5:00 p.m.

Several interpretive and living history events are held at Old Fort Johnson each year. In one of the many elegant rooms found in this frontier mansion, a musician prepares to play on a portable keyboard instrument based on those of the mid-18th century. Courtesy Old Fort Johnson.

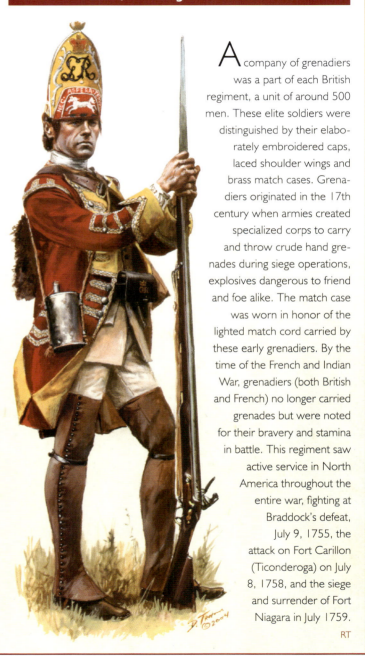

British Grenadier, 44th Regiment of Foot 1759

A company of grenadiers was a part of each British regiment, a unit of around 500 men. These elite soldiers were distinguished by their elaborately embroidered caps, laced shoulder wings and brass match cases. Grenadiers originated in the 17th century when armies created specialized corps to carry and throw crude hand grenades during siege operations, explosives dangerous to friend and foe alike. The match case was worn in honor of the lighted match cord carried by these early grenadiers. By the time of the French and Indian War, grenadiers (both British and French) no longer carried grenades but were noted for their bravery and stamina in battle. This regiment saw active service in North America throughout the entire war, fighting at Braddock's defeat, July 9, 1755, the attack on Fort Carillon (Ticonderoga) on July 8, 1758, and the siege and surrender of Fort Niagara in July 1759. RT

Painting by Don Troiani, Historical Image Bank.

Johnson Hall State Historic Site

By the early 1760s, Sir William Johnson had become the most prestigious individual in the Mohawk Valley, living the life of an English country gentleman. War hero, baronet, superintendent of Indian affairs, and the wealthiest landowner in the Mohawk Valley, he turned over occupancy of Fort Johnson to his son John and moved into a new mansion a few miles distant. Offered the position of royal governor of the colony of New York, he turned it down, preferring to continue in his role as liaison to the Mohawks.

What is easily forgotten is that the end of hostilities between Britain and France in North America did not mark the end of the French and Indian War. It continued in Europe and elsewhere, and it continued in North America. France's cession to England of its claims in America did nothing to satisfy the claims of the American Indian. The Native American was the odd man out. Promises were made, promises were broken, and the Indian fought back. Johnson's expertise and influence in Indian affairs would become an invaluable commodity over the next dozen years.

Until 1763, Johnson, still nominally in charge of Indian affairs, was actually responsible to the commander-in-chief of British forces in America, Lord Jeffery Amherst. Amherst — who disagreed over the need to lavish gifts upon the Indians — and Johnson clashed at every turn. When Amherst was recalled in 1763, he was replaced by General Thomas Gage, who pretty much gave Johnson free rein. Johnson was able to negotiate agreements with the Indians, but he never knew just how much support he would receive from the home government in making sure those agreements were honored. Representing the Crown as well as he could, he continued to be a busy man.

His new home, Johnson Hall, was of wood construction made to look like stone. The grounds were dotted with service buildings, among which were barns, a blacksmith shop, an Indian store, a mill, and two westward-facing stone forts guarding the aspect with the greatest exposure. Continuing in the hospi-

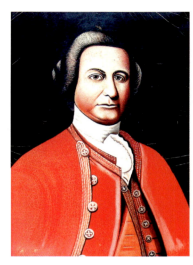

Portrait of Sir William Johnson. Photo by Randy Patten.

Johnson Hall from the front. The imposing stone blockhouses flank the main house on each side. Photo courtesy NYS OPRHP.

Johnson Hall, view from the rear courtyard. Photo courtesy Johnson Hall SHS.

The dining room at Johnson Hall, furnished to look as it did when Molly Brant and Sir William Johnson lived there, based on an inventory taken at the time of Sir William's death in 1774. Photo courtesy NYS OPRHP.

table tradition of Fort Johnson, Johnson Hall graced frequent sizable gatherings both for family and friends and for diplomatic conferences involving the Iroquois. No matter how important an Englishman Johnson had become, the Iroquois always knew he was their last best hope. To them he was Warraghiyagey. They trusted him. He was one of them. He listened to their grievances, and he did the best he could to resolve them.

It was at one of those conferences with the Iroquois in 1774, a particularly contentious gathering about yet more failed promises, that Johnson collapsed and died. The property and title passed to his son Sir John, a Loyalist who fled to Canada during the Revolution, at which time Johnson Hall was confiscated by the state and sold at auction. American soldiers who came to arrest Sir John at the start of the Revo-

Johnson Hall in 1865. Courtesy Johnson Hall SHS.

lution were afterwards court-martialed by order of George Washington. Sir John having fled, the soldiers arrested his wife Mary, got drunk, and looted the property. (A damaged stair rail remains today as testimony to their actions.) Washington felt punishment necessary to placate the Iroquois, who remained devoted to Sir William and his memory. ■ SB

The *Liaisons Plaisantes* ensemble plays period music at a Johnson Hall living history event. Courtesy Johnson Hall SHS.

● **VISITING JOHNSON HALL SHS**
139 Hall Ave, Johnstown, NY 12095
(518) 762-8712 / Fax: (518) 762-2330
www.friendsofjohnsonhall.org
• Open May through October. Check websites for hours, events and other information.

Molly Brant • Koñwatsiātsiaiéñni

Koñwatsiātsiaiéñni • Gonwatsijayenni
Degonwadonti • Molly Brant

Take your pick. History books use any of the four names or spellings, although most simply call her Molly Brant. Her native Mohawk name, Koñwatsiātsiaiéñni, translates as, "someone lends her a flower".

Sister of Thayendanegea (Joseph Brant). Possible granddaughter of Theyanoguin (King Hendrick). Mother to eight of Sir William Johnson's children. Chatelaine of Johnson Hall. Matriarch of the Wolf clan. Respected Iroquois diplomat. Steadfast Loyalist.

As William Johnson moved freely between two worlds, so did Molly Brant. He was attracted to her, so the story goes, when she, a carefree sixteen-year-old, accepted a challenge to participate in a riding competition between Mohawks and British officers. From 1759 until Johnson's death in 1774, they lived as man and wife in their two Mohawk Valley homes. When Johnson died, she moved with her children to Canajoharie where she resumed her role as a leader of the Mohawk nation. An active supporter of the British during the American Revolution, she fled to Canada after the war, where she was rewarded for her fidelity with a home and pension.

After a visit to Johnson Hall, an Englishwoman wrote:

Her features are fine and beautiful; her complexion clear and olive-tinted… She was quiet in demeanour… and possessed of a calm dignity that bespoke a native pride and consciousness of power. She seldom imposed herself into the picture, but no one was in her presence without being aware of her.

A remarkable woman by any name or by any measure. SB

Fort Klock Historic Restoration

The Johannes Klock house is furnished with period items typical of the mid-18th century. Photo courtesy Randy Patten.

Fort Klock, a fortified stone house and trading post built in the Mohawk Valley by Palatine immigrant Johannes Klock in 1750, is a testament to the ironies of war.

Palatines were Germans who had been living in an area of 17th-century Europe that had suffered repeatedly at the hands of the French. They appealed for relief to the government of Britain, who accepted them as refugees, hoping to utilize the Protestantism of the Palatines to increase anti-Catholic sentiment. When the ranks of the refugees swelled into the thousands, Britain decided it could no longer support them, and many of the Palatines were shipped to America to be employed as indentured labor in the production of naval stores. With the failure of that enterprise, the Palatines were left destitute. From the Hudson Valley where they had first settled, many moved into the Mohawk Valley, encouraged by Governor William Burnet of New York who commented, "These will be a barrier to sudden incursions of the French." Having fled thousands of miles to a new continent to escape French persecution in Europe, the Palatines found themselves at the onset of the French and Indian War installed on the frontier as a safety net against the French in the Mohawk Valley.

Rufus Grider did this painting of Fort Klock and the engravings on its stonework in 1886. Courtesy New York State Library, Manuscripts and Special Collections.

The L-shaped house that Johannes Klock built reflects his awareness of the threat and his concern for his family's safety. With substantial limestone walls nearly two-feet thick resting on a foundation of solid bedrock, loopholes at intervals on all sides allowing for protective musket fire, a spring supplying a constant source of fresh water bubbling up through the solid rock basement floor, the house presented a formidable challenge for any would-be attackers. Since it was a trading post as well as a private home, a sheltered cove along the riverbank adjacent to the house provided safe anchorage for the bateau traffic that plied the river between Schenectady and the Oneida Carry.

The defensive strengths of Fort Klock were not tested during the French and Indian War, but a Revolutionary War battle with echoes of the earlier war was fought in the immediate vicinity. Sir William Johnson's Loyalist son, Sir John Johnson, bitter about being forced earlier

"Map of the northern parts of New York," a detail showing the Hudson and Mohawk Rivers and Schoharie Creek, c. 1758. This large pen-and-ink and watercolor map shows the Hudson River from Albany to Fort Edward, the Mohawk and Hoosic rivers, Schoharie Creek, nearby roads and villages, some landowners and also includes descriptive notes — some indicating the number of families in each village. Courtesy Library of Congress.

From the Historic American Buildings Survey/Historic American Engineering Record comes this photo of Fort Klock by Stanley P. Mixon, made on June 15, 1940. This is a general view of the site looking toward the Mohawk River, seen in the distance. The house is just to the right of the barn at center. Courtesy Library of Congress.

to abandon the Johnson property, in 1780 led 1,000 British troops on a raid designed to wreak havoc and destruction in the Mohawk Valley. Neighbors gathered inside Fort Klock, and, although the structure itself was not a factor in the battle, it is reported that one of those seeking protection inside shot a mounted British soldier, the riderless horse approached the house, and a camp kettle was removed from the horse and became a Klock family heirloom. Confronted by militia near Fort Klock, Johnson's forces were driven back and forced to flee the area.

Today, Fort Klock is the centerpiece of a thirty-acre restoration which includes a 19th-century school, a blacksmith shop, and a colonial Dutch barn. Its proximity to Old Fort Johnson, also completed in 1750 and about a half-hour drive away, provides an opportunity for a visitor to make immediate comparisons between two exactly contemporaneous homes representing two distinct cultures, economic standards and political circles. ■ SB

VISITING FORT KLOCK

Fort Klock Historic Restoration

Route 5; 2 Mi. E. of St. Johnsville
PO Box 42, St. Johnsville, NY 13452
518-568-7779
www.fortklockrestoration.org
and www.fortklock.org

- Hours are Memorial Day–Columbus Day, Tuesday–Sunday 9 a.m.–5 p.m.

Johannes Klock's stone house as it is seen today. Photo courtesy Randy Patten.

Powder horns

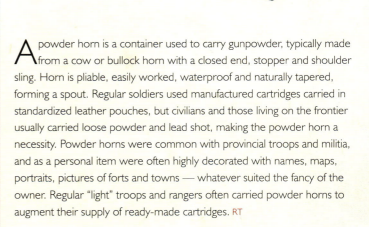

Powder horn with hand-drawn map of the Hudson River, Mohawk River, Niagara region and Lake Ontario in New York Province and the British royal arms, 1757–1760, probably belonging to a provincial soldier. Courtesy the Library of Congress.

Robert Rogers's powder horn, inscribed "Robert Rodgers / his horn Fort Wm henry June 13 1756." Picture courtesy Fort Ticonderoga Museum. (Photos are not shown in scale to each other.)

A powder horn is a container used to carry gunpowder, typically made from a cow or bullock horn with a closed end, stopper and shoulder sling. Horn is pliable, easily worked, waterproof and naturally tapered, forming a spout. Regular soldiers used manufactured cartridges carried in standardized leather pouches, but civilians and those living on the frontier usually carried loose powder and lead shot, making the powder horn a necessity. Powder horns were common with provincial troops and militia, and as a personal item were often highly decorated with names, maps, portraits, pictures of forts and towns — whatever suited the fancy of the owner. Regular "light" troops and rangers often carried powder horns to augment their supply of ready-made cartridges. RT

Fort Stanwix National Monument

The story of Fort Stanwix is the story of the Oneida Carry, the vital link in the Hudson River to Lake Ontario water passage. The Oneida Carry, also known as "The Great Carrying Place" (one of several in the Northeast!), was the portage connecting the eastward flowing Mohawk River and the westward flowing Wood Creek. Seasonally varying between one and six miles, this short stretch of land carried a strategic significance far in excess of its abbreviated length. Control of the portage translated into control of the entire route from Albany to Lake Ontario and beyond. Fort Stanwix was the culmination of a long struggle for that control.

With the Carry being situated squarely in the heart of Iroquoia, the arrival in the early 17th century of the Europeans gave the Iroquois the ability to initiate fur trade in both directions, with the French in the west and the Dutch and then the English in the east. In 1727 the English, already counting on their friendship with the Iroquois, extended their influence with construction of a fortified trading post at Oswego on Lake Ontario. Having already engaged in two previous colonial wars with the French and their non-Iroquois Indian allies, this provocation ratcheted up tension and animosity between the two European powers. Recognizing the potential military significance of the Carry, the British constructed stockades at either end of Oneida Lake.

As trade increased over the next 25 years, so did the British presence on the portage. Where there was trade and there were people, there was money to be made. Transporting goods across the portage became a thriving industry. The connecting road was improved. Wagoners and their families moved in.

With the onset of war with France in the 1750s, the need to keep the pipeline open to Oswego became critical. The vulnerability of the portage made it a prime target for the French, and with that increased threat came an increased need to provide for its defense. Fort Williams and Fort Bull were constructed at either end of the portage. When Fort Bull was destroyed in a March 1756 attack, it was replaced by Fort Wood Creek. Fort Williams was replaced by a stronger facility, Fort Craven. Fort Newport was added

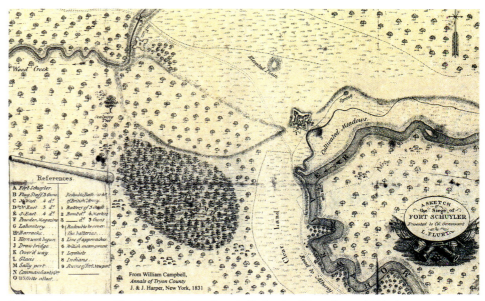

"A Sketch of the Siege of Fort Schuyler" from Campbell's *Annals of Tryon County*, 1831, showing the fort's strategic location between the Mohawk River and Wood Creek. Fort Stanwix, renamed Fort Schuyler by the Americans, was unsuccessfully besieged during the Revolutionary War by British forces. The fort was abandoned in 1781 after the fort was damaged by flood and fire, and was not rebuilt until the modern reconstruction by the National Park Service in the 1970s. Courtesy Ron Toelke.

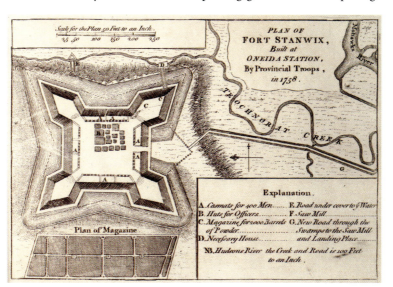

"Plan of Fort Stanwix Built at Oneida Station By Provincial Troops in 1758," from John Rocque, *A Set of Plans and Forts in America, Reduced from Actual Surveys*, London, Mary Ann Rocque, 1763. Courtesy New York State Library.

The site of Fort Stanwix c.1850, from Benson Lossing's *Pictorial Field Book of the Revolution*.

● VISITING FORT STANWIX

Fort Stanwix National Monument (National Park Service)
112 E Park Street, Rome, NY 13440   315-338-7730
• For visitor information go to www.nps.gov/fost/

Above, an illustration of Fort Stanwix as it looked in 1777. At left, an aerial view of the fort as it appears today, located in downtown Rome, New York — all of the fort's buildings are reconstructions. Both courtesy of the National Park Service, Fort Stanwix National Monument.

to protect a dam that had been built to help control the seasonal flow of water at the Wood Creek end of the portage. The British investment here in men, money, and materials was significant. Unfortunately for the British, however, the fall of the military complex at Oswego in the fall of 1756 changed everything.

Afraid that the French would follow up that success with an attack at the portage, General Webb panicked — the same General Webb who would fail to provide relief for the besieged Fort William Henry the following year. He ordered a complete withdrawal to German Flatts and the destruction of every British facility between the Mohawk River and Wood Creek. German Flatts was laid waste the following year, opening up the Mohawk Valley to potential invasion by the French, an invasion that might have come in 1758 but for the threat to Fort Carillon by English forces. When French forces pulled back to help in Fort Carillon's defense, the British moved back to the control the Oneida Carry and built Fort Stanwix (named for its first commander, Brigadier John Stanwix), at the portage, thereby regaining their control of the HudsonRiver to Lake Ontario connection. The fort, a substantial earthwork construction surrounded by a palisade and ditch, saw no action during the remainder of the French and Indian War. Its glory days as a player in the American Revolution lay ahead. ■ SB

New York provincial soldier 1758

New York raised troops for each year of the war. Every county in New York was expected to provide a quota of men to serve in the Provincial Army, which would then become part of the British Army in North America. The New York Provincials took part in all the major, and most of the minor, engagements of the war in New York, and also saw service in New England, Canada, and Cuba. The New York provincial troops were clothed, armed, supplied and paid by the Province of New York. Different colored uniforms were worn each year, beginning with blue coats faced red and later a coat of a green color resembling modern olive drab. The finer-quality coats of the officers were a darker green with silver lace. This soldier wears the 1758 clothing issue — green coats faced with green. In that year hats were cut down to a 2 ½ inch brim. They were armed with "Brown Bess" muskets and black or brown leather accoutrements. RT

Painting by Don Troiani, Historical Image Bank.

Fort Brewerton Blockhouse

The capitulation of Montréal in September, 1760, marking the end of fighting between France and England in North America, did not end the war. The British drove the French from the continent, but fighting continued in Europe, the Caribbean and elsewhere, and no resolution to the Indian question had been found. Native Americans were truly the odd men out. Had the colonists not fought for the right to claim the Ohio Country? Were they not free to spill over the Appalachian Mountains and take over the land they had won from France? Were not the Indians a mere speed bump to the voracious territorial appetite of the British colonists? It seemed to the colonists that the answer to all these questions should be a resounding, "Yes."

Native American tribes were not going to concede without a struggle. The spring of 1763 saw tribes in the Great Lakes area and the Ohio Country rise up against the influx of white settlers in Pontiac's Rebellion. The Indians burned forts, and settlers by the hundreds were killed or captured. As for the Iroquois role in all of this, a November, 1763 letter from Sir William Johnson to the London authorities explained the source of their grievances: "The grand matter of concern to all the Six Nations… is the occupying a chain of small Posts on the communication thro' their country to Lake Ontario…; in order to obtain permission for erecting these posts, they were promised they should be demolished at the

Fort Brewerton as it would have appeared in 1759. Courtesy Fort Brewerton Historical Society.

Rebben Smith decorated his powder horn with maps and pictures related to the main areas of conflict in New York. "Fort Brwton" (Brewerton) is just to the right of "Lake Onyd" (Lake Oneida). Many other forts and towns are shown. The illustration was done by archeologist Robert Hartley in 1937. Courtesy the Margaret Reaney Memorial Library.

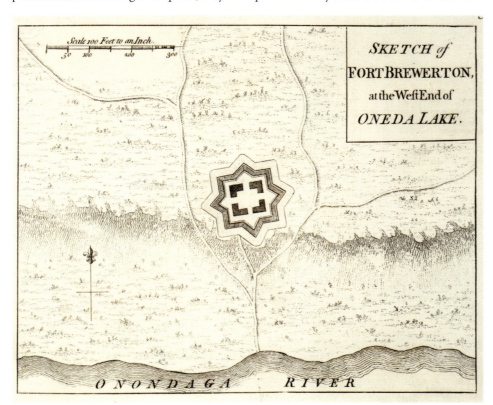

Fort Brewerton, John Rocque, *A Set of Plans and Forts in America, Reduced from Actual Surveys,* London, Mary Ann Rocque, 1763. In the interior were four timber blockhouses, each able to house 100 men, together with their equipment and supplies. Courtesy New York State Library.

VISITING FORT BREWERTON
Fort Brewerton Historical Society
P. O. Box 392, 9 US Route 11,
Brewerton, NY 13029
315-668-8801
www.fortbrewerton.org

end of the war…[T]he same has not been performed… which they look upon as the first steps to enslave them and invade their properties." One of the posts specifically cited by Johnson in this letter was Fort Brewerton.

When the British reclaimed control of the Mohawk Valley/Lake Ontario water route, Fort Brewerton was erected at the west end of Lake Oneida to serve primarily as a communications link between Fort Stanwix and Fort Ontario. Completed in 1759 under the supervision of Captain George Brewerton, the fort's footprint was an 8-pointed star, each of the projections extending about 30 feet, the resulting 480-foot parapet defended by four 3-lb. swivel guns. Girding the perimeter was an earthen embankment and 20-foot high loopholed stockade, all surrounded by a protective ditch.

That first cold winter of 1759–1760 saw Fort Brewerton playing host to a detachment of 30 Rangers under the command of Captain Joseph Waite. In February, Captain Waite made a recruiting trip east and reported with 73 additional recruits to Jeffery Amherst at Albany, who ordered him to Fort Ontario with those men and the 30 awaiting him at Fort Brewerton to prepare to take part in the final assault on Montréal.

Fort Brewerton's usefulness as a military installation had passed. The garrison was maintained from the collapse of New France until the end of Pontiac's Rebellion, but in 1767, in accordance with treaty obligations, it was dismantled. The original earthworks of the fort still exist and are adjacent to the reconstruction of a 1790s blockhouse named for Oliver Stevens, the first European settler in Brewerton. The blockhouse accommodates a museum containing a collection of period artifacts. ■ SB

The reconstructed Oliver Stevens blockhouse in Brewerton. Stevens operated a tavern here for the bateaux men who traveled the route and traded with the Indians for furs. Photo courtesy Fort Brewerton Historical Society.

Eastern Woodland Indian (Iroquois) during the French & Indian War

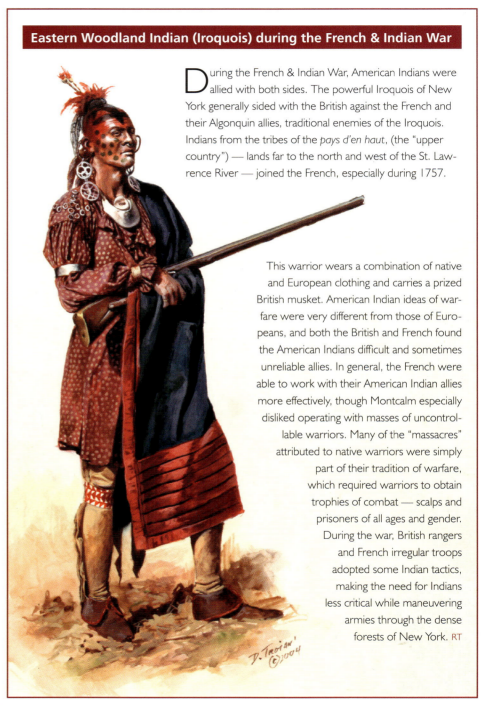

During the French & Indian War, American Indians were allied with both sides. The powerful Iroquois of New York generally sided with the British against the French and their Algonquin allies, traditional enemies of the Iroquois. Indians from the tribes of the *pays d'en haut*, (the "upper country") — lands far to the north and west of the St. Lawrence River — joined the French, especially during 1757.

This warrior wears a combination of native and European clothing and carries a prized British musket. American Indian ideas of warfare were very different from those of Europeans, and both the British and French found the American Indians difficult and sometimes unreliable allies. In general, the French were able to work with their American Indian allies more effectively, though Montcalm especially disliked operating with masses of uncontrollable warriors. Many of the "massacres" attributed to native warriors were simply part of their tradition of warfare, which required warriors to obtain trophies of combat — scalps and prisoners of all ages and gender. During the war, British rangers and French irregular troops adopted some Indian tactics, making the need for Indians less critical while maneuvering armies through the dense forests of New York. RT

Painting by Don Troiani, Historical Image Bank.

Lakes to Locks Passage

The lengthened sheet of the Champlain stretched from the frontiers of Canada, deep within the borders of the neighboring province of New York, forming a natural passage across half the distance that the French were compelled to master in order to strike their enemies. Near its southern termination, it received the contributions of another lake, whose waters were so limpid as to have been exclusively selected by the Jesuit missionaries to perform the typical purification of baptism, and to obtain for it the title of lake "du Saint Sacrement…."

Winding its way among countless islands, and imbedded in mountains, the "holy lake" extended a dozen leagues still farther to the south. With the high plain that there interposed itself to the further passage of water, commenced a portage of as many miles, which conducted the adventurer to the banks of the Hudson, at a point where, with the usual obstructions of the rapids…the river became navigable to the tide.

J.F. Cooper, Last of the Mohicans

One might argue with the fanciful manipulation of history that romanticizes James Fenimore Cooper's account of the fall of Fort William Henry in *The Last of the Mohicans*, but it is hard to imagine a finer depiction of the Albany-Montréal waterway that is now embraced by the Lakes to Locks Passage.

During the French and Indian War, forces might leave the staging area of Crailo and head north to Fort Edward on the Hudson before setting out along the portage to Lake George. Until William Johnson's arrival at the head of an army of 2,000 in 1755, Lake George had been known by the dulcet French *Lac du Saint-Sacrement* (Lake of the Holy Sacrament). The Iroquois called it *Andiatarocte* (The Lake Shut In). Johnson, however, rechristened it Lake George for the reigning Hanoverian English monarch George II, a name Cooper himself referred to as "vulgar," and which prompted him to coin an entirely new name for the crystalline lake, *Horican* (The Tail of the Lake), in his novel. From his vantage point at the southern terminus of the lake, Cooper beheld a shimmering surface "indented with numberless bays, embellished by fantastic headlands, and dotted with countless islands."

But Lake George it was and would remain. For the next several years, vast flotillas of bateaux carrying massive armies would ply its waters — Montcalm's besieging forces heading south in 1757 to invest Fort William Henry, Abercromby's proceeding north in 1758 toward Forts Carillon and St. Frédéric only to return in all out flight, and Amherst's in 1759 making a second attempt with much greater success. Rogers's Rangers would utilize its waters and frozen winter surfaces for his lightning raids into the north country, as would the French coming south in an early March 1757 hit-and-run assault on Fort William Henry.

After consolidating his gains and securing Carillon and St. Frédéric on Lake Champlain in 1759, Amherst would, in 1760, turn over the leadership of those forces to General Haviland for the final push. Haviland and his army of 3,500 would advance the length of Lake Champlain to where it funneled into the Richelieu River, drive the French from their fort at Île-aux-Noix, and continue down the Richelieu to join the forces of Amherst and Murray as they converged on Montréal.

This ebbing and flowing of both British and French troop movements along the Richelieu River-Lake Champlain-Lake George-Hudson River corridor capitalized on the advantages of 18th-century travel by water and accentuated the strategic importance of New York's abundant waterways.

Lakes to Locks Passage

Lakes to Locks Passage is a success story demonstrating that productive intergovernmental cooperation is possible. Since 2000, community, county, state, and national governments have shared their resources to create a remarkable interconnected pathway linking the Mohawk and St. Lawrence Rivers. In 2002, Lakes to Locks Passage was named an "All-American Road" by the Federal Highway Administration because of its historic and recreational attractions for visitors. Along with the specific sites included in this guide, travelers experience the region's historic, natural, cultural, and recreational assets through close contact with the region's waterways — the Champlain Canal, Hudson River, Lake George, and Lake Champlain in New York, and the Chambly Canal and Richelieu River in Québec. Opportunities abound for outdoor enthusiasts to get "up-close-and-personal" with the breathtaking natural beauty of the landscape, but access is readily available to everyone. Called "The Great Northeast Journey," the clearly marked Lakes to Locks Passage route enables visitors to explore the natural beauty and historic treasures of the region by foot, bicycle, boat, and car. To learn more, contact Lakes to Locks Passage, Inc. through the information listed in the resource section of the guide. ■ SB

Hikers on Cook Mountain enjoy the breathtaking view looking south over Lake George and beyond. The view is little different today than it was 250 years ago, when armies, rangers and Indians campaigned in this wide and rugged wilderness, assisted by fleets of boats moving men and supplies over the region's waterways. Photo by Gary Randorf courtesy Lakes to Locks Passage, Inc.

Crailo State Historic Site

With campaigns heading both north and west from Albany throughout the French & Indian War, British planners frequently made use of Crailo's ideal location. A 1500-acre estate in Green Bush on the east bank of the Hudson River opposite the city of Albany, Crailo (Dutch for "crows' wood") not only could accommodate large numbers of provincial soldiers, but it could easily be reached by units arriving by boat from the south or by foot from any of the nearby New England colonies. From Crailo, troops could then move north into the Lake George/Lake Champlain region or west into the Mohawk Valley. At the same time, the river protected the city from the inevitable disorder that would result from incursions of large numbers of rough-and-tumble New England militiamen, and it served to separate the provincials from the British troops quartered in the city. British officers billeted in Albany prepared for campaigns in relative comfort, especially when hosted by the Albany gentry, which included the Van Rensselaers, Crailo's owners and a family of respected social standing. Contemporary reports suggest that British officers, General Lyman of Connecticut (a senior provincial officer) among them, were frequent guests of the Van Rensselaers at their well-stocked dinner table.

By the time of the French and Indian War, Crailo had already experienced the terror and trauma of French and Indian attacks. Its somewhat exposed position, despite its proximity to Albany, had always made it vulnerable. Since its origins in 1642, its buildings had been rebuilt and its defenses had been strengthened a number of times, almost always in response to increased threats. During King George's War, Johannes Van Rensselaer in 1746 added a stockade and gunports in response to a series of French and Indian attacks on Green Bush which succeeded in killing or capturing 30 of Van Rensselaer's neighbors. Despite these continuous modifications, however, Crailo always remained more a fortified manor house than an actual fort.

With the onset of the French and Indian War, the grounds at Crailo quickly became a staging area for troops preparing to go off to battle. One can only imagine the chaos and turmoil created by thousands of untrained encamped colonial soldiers awaiting orders to move into the wilderness. At least one observer noted the rude behavior of those bumptious, country-bred would-be soldiers and turned it to his own use. Dr. Richard Shuckburgh, a British army surgeon and longtime friend and acquaintance of Sir William Johnson and the Van Rensselaers, was no stranger to Crailo. He rushed to tend to the wounded, including Johnson, when they arrived at a makeshift hospital at Crailo after the Battle of Lake George in 1755.

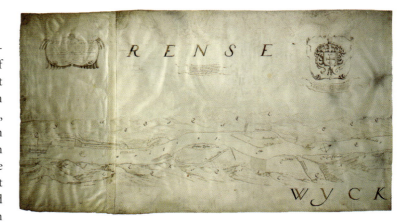

A portion of a map of Rensselaerswijck, 1632. Fort Orange is shown, as well as the future site of Crailo, on the east side of the Mauritius (Hudson) River. Courtesy New York State Library Special Collections. Below, a 17th-century delftware plate found at Crailo, courtesy of Crailo State Historic Site."

"The Trading House," the first Dutch settlement in the Albany area known as Fort Nassau, around 1615. The site of this early fort, abandoned in 1618, would become part of the vast Van Rensselaer patroonship. Crailo was established nearby. Painting by Len Tantillo, courtesy Len Tantillo.

Crailo State Historic Site in the winter of 2008. Extensive archaeology has been done on the site, uncovering thousands of artifacts spanning hundreds of years.

Known not only for his medical skills, but for his wit and his amiability, he thoroughly relished the antics of unskilled New Englanders as they tried to learn the complexities of military drill. To entertain fellow guests at the Van Rensselaer table, he penned several verses meant to ridicule the provincials' often laughable efforts. Setting those verses to a traditional mocking melody, he created *Yankee Doodle*. Little did he know that before 20 years had passed, those same unschooled provincials would adopt the song as their own and use it to mock their now British foes. SB

● VISITING CRAILO STATE HISTORIC SITE
9 ½ Riverside Avenue, Rensselaer, NY 12144 518-463-8738
- For information on hours of operation and events go to http://nysparks.state.ny.us/sites

Crailo SHS living history events present and interpret Dutch colonial culture. Above, a young woman prepares a dish of pumpkin cornmeal pancakes, a popular Dutch recipe.

The story of "Yankee Doodle"

In June 1758, British army physician Dr. Richard Shuckburgh wrote the "Yankee Doodle" lyrics while at Crailo during the French and Indian War (1755–63). Shuckburgh's words mocked the ill-equipped and undisciplined New England provincial troops, part of the large British army gathering to assault the French fort at Carillon (Ticonderoga). A guest of the Van Rensselaer family, Shuckburgh is said to have written the lyrics while sitting on the edge of a well at the rear of the house.

The now familiar tune was based on the old English nursery rhyme "Lucy Locket," also used in "The Beggar's Opera," a well-known musical play from 1728 by John Gay. "Doodle" is probably from the Dutch *dudel*, meaning fool or simpleton. A "macaroni" in 1750s England was an ultra-fashionable man who dressed and spoke in an exaggerated and affected manner — a person who "exceeded the ordinary bounds of fashion." Wealthy and fashionable young men who had been to Italy on the "Grand Tour" of the continent adopted the Italian word *maccherone* (a boorish fool) — humorously describing anything fashionable or *à la mode* as "very macaroni."

The joke to Shuckburgh was that the naive and uncouth provincials might think to emulate the extreme of fashion by simply sticking feathers in their hats.

The song was used by the British to taunt the rebel Americans during the American Revolution (1775–83), but in time the Americans took the song as their own. Many different versions of the song exist. RT

Some of the earliest lyrics:
Yankee Doodle came to town
  Riding on a pony,
Stuck a feather in his hat
  And called him Macaroni.
Brother Ephraim sold his cow
  To buy him a commission
And then he went to Canada
  To fight for the nation.
But when Ephraim he came home
  He proved an arrant coward,
He wouldn't fight the Frenchmen there
  For fear of being devoured.

This 1774 English print "What is this my son Tom" mocks the extreme and often absurd fashions of the "Macaroni."
Courtesy Wikimedia Commons.

Fort Edward and Rogers Island

In general, when pushed upon by the enemy, reserve your fire till they approach very near, which will then put them into the greatest surprise and consternation, and give you an opportunity of rushing upon them with your hatchets and cutlasses to the better advantage.

Rule #13 of Robert Rogers's 28 "Rules of Ranging"

Situated north of Albany where the Hudson River swings within 15 miles of Lake George, Fort Edward's strategic importance cannot be overstated. It commanded the southern terminus of the critical portage between the Hudson River and Lake George. Defensively, it provided the last line of protection for Albany and the lower Hudson Valley against invasion from the north. Offensively, it provided a staging area for British army campaigns into the Lake George, Lake Champlain, and Richelieu River corridor. It was that offensive advantage that attracted Independent Companies of Rangers to the island in the Hudson directly opposite the fort, an island which would also provide barracks for other provincials and a hospital for victims of smallpox.

The contrast between fort and island could not have been greater: the dedication of the fort's conventional British European military mindset against that of the island's unconventional Rogers and his unconventional military tactics. No episode illustrates this contrast better than that of the whipping post.

The gulf between the provincials and the home forces would be a recurring theme throughout the war. British professionals did not trust provincials to perform under fire; provincials dreaded nothing more than being subjected to harsh British discipline.

Quartering Rogers's hand-picked colonials in proximity to British regulars was an invitation to trouble. After two rangers were flogged at the whipping post one winter day for having stolen rum from the British, disgruntled rangers retaliated by removing the whipping post with an ax. The situation deteriorated rapidly. Colonel William Haviland, the commandant of Fort Edward, threatened courts martial; rangers threatened to leave camp; Haviland, in turn, threatened hangings for desertion; Rogers silenced everyone by taking 150 men on a midwinter raid against the French in the north country. By the time he returned, the incident, if not forgotten, had been put aside. The bottom line? Despite mutual antipathy and recriminations, the British knew they needed the cooperation of Rogers and his rangers.

Major Robert Rogers (1731–1795), from a 1776 print. Roger's service continued through Pontiac's Rebellion and the American Revolution. He led a colorful life but had a checkered career, eventually dying in poverty and obscurity.

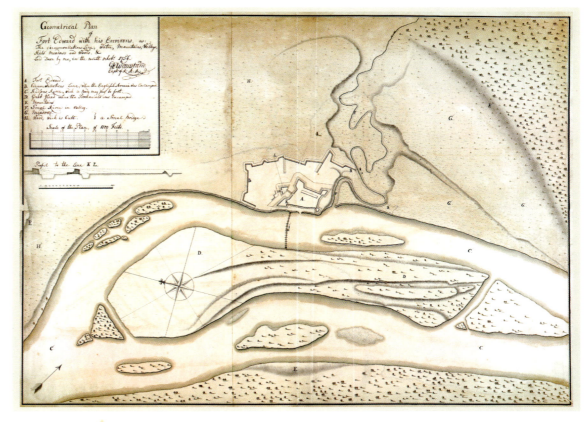

"Geometrical Plan of Fort Edward with his Environs…," October, 1756. The key lists the various parts of the fort — A is Fort Edward, D is "The Great Iland [sic] where the Provincials was Encamped" — known today as Rogers Island. Courtesy Randy Patten.

The Provincials' camp on Rogers Island, 1758. While tents were used in warm weather, soldiers in winter quarters or in more permanent camps built log huts laid out along orderly streets. Rangers in a variety of dress are seen going about typical activities in camp. Fort Edward can be seen in the distance. Courtesy Rogers Island Visitors Center.

Using the island at Fort Edward as their base, Rangers embarked upon assignments that have achieved legendary status — the two Battles on Snowshoes, Rogers's escape at what is known as Rogers Slide, and the destruction deep in enemy territory of the Indian village at Saint-François (Odanak), Québec. Defying impossible weather conditions, conducting wilderness operations behind enemy lines, enduring unimaginable physical deprivation and danger, they established a standard for exemplary military conduct.

After 250 years, Rogers Island at Fort Edward continues to be honored as the birthplace of today's United States special forces, especially the Army Rangers. Rogers's original 28 "Rules of Ranging" have been continually modified to meet changing conditions, but they are still used as part of training today to reflect the fundamental philosophy of an elite, quick-strike, special forces mentality. ■ SB

Rogers Island today in Fort Edward, New York. Photo courtesy Randy Patten.

● **VISITING ROGERS ISLAND**
Rogers Island Visitors Center
11 Rogers Island Drive (off Rte. 197) –
PO Box 208, Fort Edward, NY 12828
518-747-3693
www.rogersisland.org
• Wednesday – Saturday 10 a.m. – 4 p.m.
Sunday 1 p.m. – 4 p.m.
Open daily June through August

His Majesty's Independent Companies of Rangers 1758

Formed in the winter of 1755 at Fort William Henry and made famous by New Hampshire-born Robert Rogers, "His Majesty's Independent Companies of Rangers" wore distinctive green clothing adapted for operations in the dense forests of New York. After the surrender of Fort William Henry in August 1757, the Rangers were stationed on Rogers Island near Fort Edward, where they practiced tactics embodied as "Rogers' Rules of Ranging." The Rangers became the British army's chief scouting and raiding force during the war, fighting two bloody winter battles on snowshoes — one in 1757 and another in 1758 in the Lake George and Ticonderoga region. They were active throughout the war, raiding the Saint-Francis Indian settlement in Québec in October, 1759 and taking over control of Detroit from the French at the close of the war. RT

Painting by Don Troiani. Historical Image Bank.

Lake George Battlefield

British plans for 1755 included an attack on Lake Champlain's Fort St. Frédéric. William Johnson's army of 1600 provincials accompanied by 200 Mohawks under the leadership of the venerable Theyanoguin (Chief Hendrick) were to move down Lake George to Lake Champlain and the French fort. The French, aware of British intentions, were determined to stop the campaign before it could get started. Baron Dieskau, newly arrived from France, left most of his regulars at Carillon and headed south with a mixed force of 200 regular grenadiers, 600 Canadian militia, and 700 Indians to attack what he thought was a lightly defended and vulnerable Fort Edward, then known as Fort Lyman. Destroying the fort and its war supplies would, he knew, effectively throttle any immediate British activity on the lakes.

Arriving in the vicinity of Fort Lyman, Dieskau learned from scouts that the fort was better defended than had previously been thought, and that his complement of Abenaki and Caughnawaga Mohawks (Mohawks converted to Catholicism and the French cause) would not attack a fort, no matter how lightly defended. They would, however, participate in an attack on Johnson's encampment at the head of the lake. Johnson's intelligence, at the same time, informed him of the presence of enemy in the area, and he determined to send reinforcements to Fort Lyman. The first phase of the Battle of Lake George — since known as the Bloody Morning Scout — would involve the collision of those forces on the newly constructed supply road from Fort Lyman to Lake George.

On the morning of September 8, 1200 men left the British encampment headed for Fort Lyman — 1000 provincials under Colonel Ephraim Williams and Chief

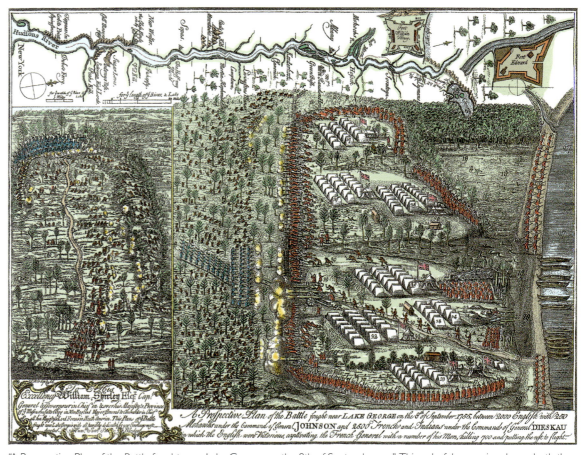

"A Prospective Plan of the Battle fought near Lake George on the 8th of September…." This colorful engraving shows both the ambush known as the "Bloody Morning Scout" at left and at right the main attack of the French (in blue) and their Indian allies against Johnson's hastily fortified camp. Above, seen sideways, is a map of the Hudson River from New York to Lake George, with inset maps of both Fort William Henry and Fort Edward. Courtesy Prints George Image Bank and Robert Whitworth.

"The Battle of Lake George" by Frederick Coffay Yohn, dramatizes the action at the height of the French attack. Colonel Williams is the figure in the blue coat. Yohn was well-known for his illustrations of military and frontier subjects. Courtesy Chapman Historical Museum.

Hendrick's 200 Mohawks. Learning of their approach from a deserter, Dieskau set a trap similar to the one that had proved fatal to Braddock on the Monongahela. Despite the deaths of both Colonel Williams and Chief Hendrick, however, the bulk of the British contingent managed to flee back to the protection of the camp, where the second phase of the battle developed.

A hastily constructed breastwork of trees, overturned wagons, and brush greeted Dieskau's pursuing force. Again encountering cannon, the Indians

"View of the Lines at Lake George, 1759," by the distinguished British army officer Captain Thomas Davies, is the earliest recorded oil painting of Lake George, done in 1774. Davies served with British forces under Amherst when they took control of the region from the French in 1759. Davies shows the military camp neatly arranged according to the "art of castramentation" on the lakeshore, with the lake receding into the distance. In the foreground a green-clad ranger talks with a seated Indian. Courtesy Fort Ticonderoga Museum.

pulled back, this time taking the Canadian militia with them. Dieskau, intent on carrying on the attack, lined up his French regulars and advanced twice against the guns, which each time cut a swath through the French lines, crippling and driving them back. A late-afternoon counterattack by the British provincials captured a wounded Baron Dieskau and drove the French from the field.

A third encounter occurred when the retreating French ran into a relief force sent from Fort Lyman. Already decimated by the day's events, the French and Indians killed in this clash were thrown into a nearby pond, earning this place the name "Bloody Pond".

In the aftermath of the battle, both sides paused to lick their respective wounds and to reinforce their forward positions. Having fled to the north end of the lake, the French constructed Fort Carillon (later Ticonderoga). The British matched them, building Fort William Henry just to the west of the battlefield — only 35 miles from Carillon. ■ SB

● **VISITING LAKE GEORGE BATTLEFIELD PARK**
Lake George Park Commission
P.O. Box 749, Fort George Road, Lake George, New York 12845   518-668-9347
Lake George Battlefield and Lake George Battlefield Picnic Area
Off U.S. Route 9, ¼ mile east of Lake George Village, New York 12845
518-668-3352   www.dec.ny.gov

This monument located in today's Battlefield Park is dedicated to the memory of Sir William Johnson, Theyanoguin (King Hendrick) and the battle fought on September 8, 1755.

Theyanoguin or "King Hendrick"

Theyanoguin, (c. 1680–1755) known to the English as Chief, or "King," Hendrick, stood irate before Governor Clinton and the New York Council on June 16, 1753. "[W]e will send up a Belt of Wampum to our Brothers the 5 Nations to acquaint them the Covenant Chain is broken between you and us." Theyanoguin's ties to the English extended far back in time. In 1710, he and three other Indian sachems — advertised as Iroquois "kings" — had traveled to London to appear before Queen Anne. Now, however, Theyanoguin accused the English of failing to honor promises to protect Mohawks from French encroachment. Their English friend William Johnson had resigned from his post as Indian agent, and they were left to deal with Albany merchants whom Theyanoguin referred to as "Devils." From this confrontation the 1754 Albany Congress was born, a gathering of colonial officials meant to provide the Iroquois with redress in an effort to reconstruct the alliance that had existed between them.

A skilled orator and powerful advocate for the Mohawks, Theyanoguin would continue to be courted by Johnson and the English and would return to the fold, but he clearly viewed the English as the lesser of two evils. In 1755 Theyanoguin would provide two hundred warriors for Johnson's proposed campaign against Fort St. Frédéric. Unfortunately, he was killed early in the Battle of Lake George, having failed in the initial moments of that encounter to convince Iroquois kin allied with the French not to raise arms against their brother Iroquois fighting with Johnson. Image courtesy Library of Congress. SB

Fort William Henry

August 7, 1757. After receiving the captured message under a flag of truce, Colonel George Munro of the 35th Regiment of Foot read the words from General Daniel Webb with dismay. No help would be coming from Fort Edward. The only hope of the British defenders at Fort William Henry had vanished.

In a display of classic siegecraft, Montcalm's army was in the process of rendering Fort William Henry virtually helpless. Despite the fort's substantial fortifications, no 18th-century wilderness fort could withstand a prolonged period of artillery bombardment. With no relief in sight, Munro would have to ask for terms of surrender. He could not capitulate quite yet, however. The formal conventions of 18-century war would not permit it. To receive honorable terms, enough of his forces had to be killed and enough damage had to be inflicted on the fort to demonstrate that he had put up a good fight.

After the 1755 Battle of Lake George, the British had decided to consolidate their position at the south end of Lake George by con-

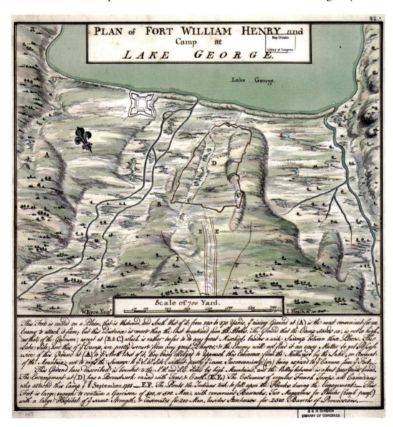

A contemporary French map shows Fort William Henry [A] and the large camp of the provincial troops [C]. The map also shows Montcalm's siege trenches and cannon batteries (upper left, B, E, F, G) and surrounding forces (I, K, H). The map uses the French name for Lake George, Lac St. Sacrament. Courtesy Fort William Henry Museum.

structing a fort to protect the terminus of the new wagon road between Lake George and Fort Edward and to provide a base of operations from which to launch raids north into the Champlain Valley. In two short months, under the watchful eye of military engineer Captain William Eyre, an imposing earth-and-timber fort was erected. The 30-foot thick, 15-foot high, horizontally-laid timber walls were filled with rubble and earth excavated from the 30-foot wide ditch that encompassed the three sides of the fort not facing the lake. To break through those defenses would take an impressive display of firepower.

In the summer of 1757, Montcalm headed south on Lake George with an army of 8,000 men— 6,000 regular French soldiers and militia and 1,800 Indians from 39 tribes. Braddock's defeat on the Monongahela and the fall of the forts at Oswego had proved to be an irresistible attraction for recruitment. Indian volunteers from the *pays d'en haut* had appeared in large

This period British map and key give a good sense of the terrain around the fort and the large entrenched camp of the provincial troops, separated from each other by low, marshy ground. Courtesy Library of Congress.

● VISITING
FORT WILLIAM HENRY
Fort William Henry Museum
Canada Street, Lake George, NY 12845
518-668-5471 www.fwhmuseum.com

- Open May to October, 9 a.m. – 6 p.m. daily. For complete visitor information go to website

numbers, all expecting to achieve glory in battle and to return to their villages with captive prisoners and plunder.

True to the form of European siege warfare, when Montcalm had established his army before the fort, he offered Colonel Munro an opportunity to surrender. Following the expected refusal, the French began digging a series of trenches toward, and then parallel to, the fort in order to bring cannons within range. After having watched three days of preparatory digging and then enduring three more days of relentless artillery fire, and knowing Webb would not be sending a relief force, on August 9, Munro accepted terms of surrender. These terms permitted his men to march back to Fort Edward with their personal effects, personal arms, one brass fieldpiece symbolizing their courage, and with their colors (flags) intact.

What happened next should have been no surprise to Montcalm. It had already happened at Oswego. He had seen what happened to prisoners of the Ottawas at Fort St. Frédéric. He knew that his Indian allies fought primarily to distinguish themselves in battle and to mark their valor with scalps and prisoners. He was aware that they fought by their own rules, and did not respond to European military customs and discipline.

When denied their promised plunder, the Indians decided to take by force what they felt they had earned. Estimates of the number of British killed, scalped, and taken prisoner vary widely, but the ensuing carnage changed the war in two ways. Feeling betrayed by the French, Indian warriors never again showed up in such large numbers, and the British, failing to get the protection promised by Montcalm, never again offered the French honorable terms of war. ■ SB

This dramatic 19th-century engraving depicts Montcalm trying in vain to stop the Indian attack on the surrendered British garrison as they began their march back to Fort Edward. Courtesy Library of Congress.

The recreated Fort William Henry sits on its orignal location on the south shore of Lake George. Photograph by Carl Heilman II, courtesy Fort William Henry Museum.

New Jersey Provincial Regiment "The Jersey Blues" 1757

Known as the "Jersey Blues" for their blue coats with red facings, 500 men of this provincial unit were sent to Oswego in 1755 to improve the fortifications and garrison the fort. They suffered many casualties as a result of Montcalm's attack on Oswego in 1756. The regiment was brought up to strength in 1757 and five companies of Jersey Blues were sent to Fort William Henry, led by Col. John Parker. About 300 were sent on a reconnaissance in force up Lake George and were ambushed near Sabbath Day Point while aboard their boats on July 23, 1757. Three-quarters of the men were killed or captured that day, and the rest were taken when Fort William Henry was surrendered to Montcalm's army in August.

The regiment was mustered again, and served with Abercromby's army against Fort Carillon in 1758 and remained in the Lake George region in 1759. In 1760 they advanced into Canada and in 1762 were part of the British expedition against Havana, Cuba. The Jersey Blues fought throughout the American Revolution as the 1st New Jersey Regiment. RT

Painting by Don Troiani, Historical Image Bank.

Lake George Shipwrecks

Moving the masses of men and material needed for an 18th-century military campaign was never an easy matter in the Northeast. Horses and oxen had to be acquired, managed, and fed. Roads through heavily-forested areas had to be constructed and kept in good repair, as did the vehicles which would travel over them. Whenever possible water routes were the paths of choice. Rivers, streams, and lakes became highways. Boats appeared in all shapes and sizes and were designed and adapted to local conditions. Preserved in the cold depths well beneath the surface of Lake George are relics of that marine past. In one of the most unusual settings imaginable for a "museum," visitors today (who are qualified divers) can view 250-year-old remains of vessels that played a central role in the conflict on the lakes.

A March, 1757 surprise attack on Fort William Henry demonstrated both the advantages and vulnerabilities afforded by the lake. Although boat traffic was limited seasonally, the thick ice formed by frigid Northeast temperatures created a surface ideal for the rapid movement of lightly-armed foot soldiers. A force of 1500 French, Canadians, and Indians outfitted with snowshoes, skates, and ice creepers, crossed the frozen lake and harassed the fort for four days. Without artillery, they had little chance of taking the fort itself, but they were able to inflict heavy damage on outbuildings and the destruction of stores of hundreds of watercraft stockpiled along the shore. Months would pass before the fort's bateaux, so vital to the transport of troops, could be replaced.

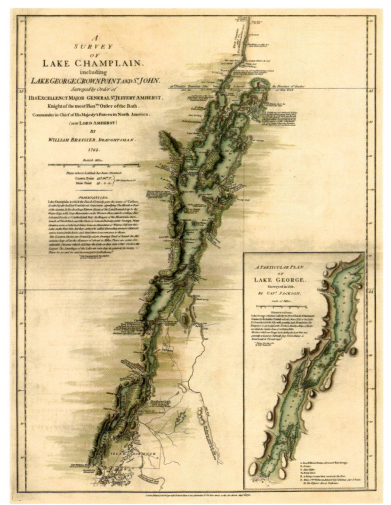

"A Survey of Lake Champlain, including Lake George, Crown Point and St. John," by William Brassier, 1762. This map, published in 1776, summarizes the progressive British control of these waterways between 1756 and 1762. Tributary rivers and streams, depth soundings, distance scales and copious notes made this chart useful for navigation and planning purposes. Courtesy Library of Congress.

Lake George in winter. In the bitter cold New York winters, even large lakes froze over. While the armies went into winter quarters, the frozen lakes and rivers eased travel for raiding and scouting parties. Courtesy Lake George Regional Chamber of Commerce.

It had become common practice in winter to protect watercraft from the enemy by sinking them in shallow water and then raising them the following spring. Some boats at Fort William Henry had been protected in that manner. With the 1757 destruction of Fort William Henry, however, and the loss of the protection it provided — and the failed July, 1758 attack on Fort Carillon — the practice of seasonal watery interment achieved a greater urgency. In the fall of 1758, the British intentionally sank almost 300 vessels, including 260 bateaux, a sloop, some row galleys, and two radeaux. Some vessels were never retrieved; the remnants of 7 bateaux can be viewed by divers today — others remain inaccessible. Of particular interest among the others is the shell of a *radeau* (French for "raft"), the *Land Tortoise*.

Designed as a floating gun battery, the 7-sided, 52-foot *Land Tortoise* was constructed to mount 7 guns — 4 on one side, 3 on the other, staggered to prevent interference from their recoil. Powered by 26 oars, the vessel had sloping sides to protect the gun crews and oarsmen. Loaded with stones, it apparently drifted slightly before plunging to the bottom, thereby ending in water too deep to be retrieved the following spring.

Discovered by an underwater archaeological survey group, Bateaux Below, Inc., the *Land Tortoise* is one of 6 shipwrecks designated a National Historic Landmark. It is now part of the state-administered park for scuba divers. The Lake George Submerged Heritage Preserves include, as well, the 7 bateaux scuttled in 1758, a recently constructed bateau for purposes of comparison, and the 1906 motor launch *Forward*, which is the centerpiece of an underwater trail system for divers featuring several stations describing lake ecology. ■ SB

Bateaux Below's Joseph W. Zarzynski collects a measurement at the 1758 *Land Tortoise* radeau shipwreck. Photo courtesy Dr. Russ Bellico, Bateaux Below, Inc.

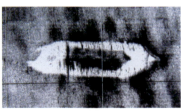

This is a Klein 595 side scan sonar image of the 1758 *Land Tortoise* radeau. The shipwreck was discovered on June 26, 1990 by Bateaux Below, Inc. during the sonar survey. Courtesy Joseph W. Zarzynski, Bateaux Below, Inc.

● **VISITING LAKE GEORGE SHIPWRECKS**
Submerged Heritage Preserve Program
NYSDEC Submerged Heritage Preserves
Region 5, Route 86, Box 296, Ray Brook, NY 12977-0296 518-897-1276
www.dec.ny.gov/lands/315.htm
Historic Lake George — Underwater
www.lakegeorgehistorical.org/(ship_2).htm
Rich Morin's Professional Scuba Center
518-761-0533 or visit www.morinsdivecenters.com

Bateaux

The difficulties of overland transportation through the New York wilderness made the movement of troops and supplies by water a critical part of any military campaign. The *bateau* (French for "boat") was the all-purpose transportation and cargo vessel (both military and civilian) used on the lakes and rivers of New York and New France. Thousands were built by British, French, and American forces during the French and Indian War, the American Revolution and the War of 1812. Double-ended with a flat bottom and a shallow draft, *bateaux* (in English "battoe" or "battoes") were sturdy, cheap to build and relatively easy for landsmen and soldiers to operate.

Bateaux were built to many sizes and specifications, but were generally 20 to 40 feet in length and similar in form — around 30 feet being the most common size. The demand for bateaux was such that many were constructed of green lumber cut from standing timber only a few days or weeks before. Bateaux were expected to last for a season or two at most, and were often sunk in shallow water to better preserve and protect them over the harsh northern winters.

Usually rowed with oars, in open water a simple mast and square sail allowed sailing with a favorable wind, one oar serving as a rudder. The typical north-south winds found on Lakes George and Champlain made sailing on these waters more practical.

French and British records attest to the ample capacity of bateaux — around three tons or in one account "8 barrels and 5 men." Some bateaux carried small swivel guns in the bow for defense, and large bateaux transported heavy artillery. An 18-pounder cannon could weigh upwards of 5,000 pounds. In 1759, Josiah Goodrich wrote that *"Each battoo Will Carry 12 barriels of flower or 9 of poark When ordered to Load And it is supposed they will have About 20 men or a few more or less."* RT

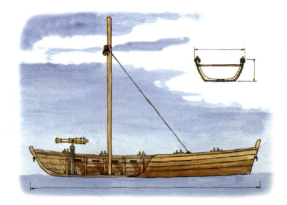

Cutaway and section views of a typical bateau with mast, mounting a swivel gun in the bow. Illustration by Robert McNamara, Art of Wilderness/Seaway Trail, Inc.

A bateau under construction. Gangs of workers assisted skilled shipwrights to rapidly construct the bateaux needed for the season's campaign. Illustration by Dahl Taylor, courtesy New York State Office of Parks, Recreation and Historic Places.

Fort Carillon/Ticonderoga

Ticonderoga. Is there a place name that better evokes a mental picture of 18th-century American colonial warfare, that resonates more in the American imagination and revolutionary tradition? Built between 1755 and 1759 by the French as Fort Carillon at the mouth of the La Chute River connecting Lake George and Lake Champlain, the fort was designed to control the portage between the lakes. In 1758 it became the battleground on which the French won their greatest American victory of the French and Indian War.

In early July, General Abercromby with 17,000 men, the largest assault force ever assembled in colonial North America, set out on Lake George in over 900 bateaux, intending to capture Fort Carillon and then move on to Fort St. Frédéric. Abercromby was ably assisted by his field commander George Augustus, Lord Howe, an officer especially popular with the provincials for his willingness to treat them with respect and lead by example.

The British encountered difficulty from the first moments of their landing. An early skirmish resulted in the death of Lord Howe. With only 3,500 defenders and inadequate provisions, Montcalm set his troops immediately to work erecting a half-mile long wooden breastwork and a formidable *abatis* (a tangled mass of fallen trees and sharpened branches) on the Heights of Carillon. Abercromby ordered a

A drawing of Ticonderoga (seen in the distance) in 1759. The trees were cleared off much of the site to provide timber for field fortifications as well as for firewood. Courtesy Library of Congress.

frontal assault on the hastily established, but impregnable, French defensive line. Observers noted the effectiveness of the *abatis* in slowing down the British advance, exposing the helpless attackers to a withering fire from the defenders. Unable to break through during a series of uncoordinated assaults lasting six hours, the British withdrew. Having lost nearly 2,000 men, the British fled in panic to the refuge of their camp at the south end of Lake George. It was a humiliating defeat for an army that had outnumbered its foe more than 4 to 1.

Late that autumn General Abercromby was replaced as Commander-in-Chief of the British army in North America by Jeffery Amherst who in 1759 led another attack on Fort Carillon. With provisions in New France scarce and no hope of reinforcement troops from France, the French planned to evacuate Carillon when it was again attacked and retreat to Québec. Thus on July 26, 1759 with the British

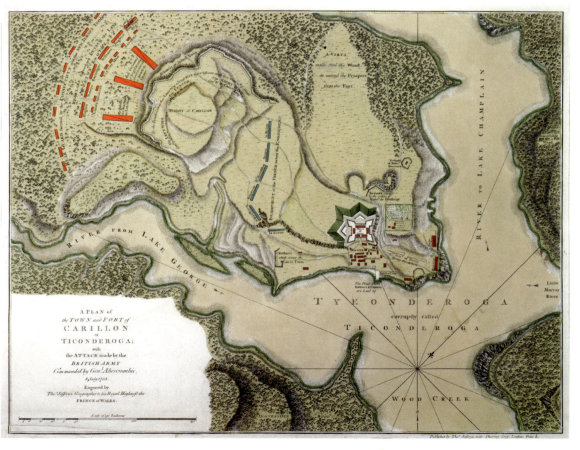

This beautiful period map of Ticonderoga presents in great detail the fort, its environs, and the strategic position it commanded between Lake George and Lake Champlain. The positions of the forces involved in the attack of July 8, 1758 (red for British and blue for French) are also shown. Courtesy Fort Ticonderoga Museum.

Fort Ticonderoga in 2007. Construction on the now completed Deborah Clarke Mars Education Center can be seen at right. Inset: the partially restored fort in 1910. In 1820, William Ferris Pell purchased the ruins of the Fort to preserve it for posterity. In 1908 Stephen and Sarah Gibbs Thompson Pell began restoration work and in 1909 Fort Ticonderoga was opened to the public. Photos courtesy Fort Ticonderoga Museum.

poised to bombard the fort with heavy cannon, the French blew up Fort Carillon's powder magazine and destroyed much of the fort. The British repaired the fort and renamed it Ticonderoga, from an Iroquois word meaning "the land between the two waters." The British would occupy this critically strategic location for the next sixteen years until it would be captured again during the surprise attack of Ethan Allen, Benedict Arnold and the Green Mountain Boys at the beginning of the American Revolution. ■ SB

Fort Ticonderoga hosts several living history and educational events each year. Here, French infantry take the field once again in July 2008, commemorating Abercromby's attack 250 years earlier. Courtesy Fort Ticonderoga Museum.

● VISITING FORT TICONDEROGA

Located on NYS RT 74, ½ mile east of NYS RT 22, Ticonderoga, NY 12883
518-585-2821
www.FortTiconderoga.org

Fort Ticonderoga
- Open daily from May through October (check website for opening and closing dates), 9:30 a.m. – 5:00 p.m.

The King's Garden
- Open daily from June through October (check website for opening and closing dates), 9:30 a.m. – 5:00 p.m.
- Go to www.FortTiconderoga.org for current admission fees and group rate information

General James Abercromby

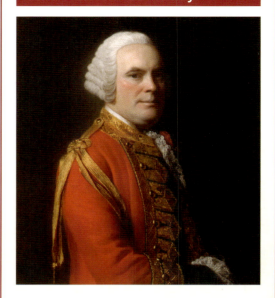

General James Abercromby (1706–1781) entered the army as a major in 1742, reaching the rank of major general in 1756. Having commanded a brigade at Halifax in 1757, Abercromby was appointed commander-in-chief of the British forces in North America in March 1758 — replacing John Campbell, 4th Earl of Loudoun, recalled to England after the failures of the 1757 campaign. A skilled organizer but a poor decision-maker, the vacillating Abercromby was called "granny," "Nabby-Cromby" or our "Booby-in-Chief" by disgruntled officers. In the summer of 1758 he led a powerful 17,000-man army to defeat with his bungled frontal attack on Montcalm's entrenched troops at Fort Carillon. The collapse of the campaign led to his dismissal in late 1758 and his replacement by Major General Jeffery Amherst. Abercromby later served in Parliament. RT

Painting by Allan Ramsay (1713–1784), courtesy Fort Ticonderoga Museum.

Crown Point State Historic Site

Outlined against the limitless sky and azure-blue waters of Lake Champlain, the sharply-etched rectangular ruins of the barracks of the British fort at Crown Point are a reminder that this bucolic landscape was once the scene of violent conflict between massive armies. Or, at least, that was the idea.

Two separate, formidable complexes of 18th-century military fortifications occupied the peninsular heights overlooking Lake Champlain. Fort St. Frédéric, constructed by the French in the 1730s, featured a four-story high stone redoubt with 12-foot thick walls and an impressive array of cannon. It was intended to intimidate all potential challengers to French rule and to control the flow of traffic on the lake. Its British successor His Majesty's Fort at Crown Point, built in 1759 to replace the shattered ruins of the fort the French had evacuated and destroyed, enclosed 7 acres with 27-foot high timber and earthwork walls surrounded by a dry ditch up to 15-feet deep cut into the bedrock. 104 guns protected its perimeter, several outworks were constructed and it could support a garrison of 4,000 men. Both fortresses were amply prepared for battles that never came.

Fort St. Frédéric had been an elusive target for the British from the very beginning, from before the first British regulars arrived. In 1755 General Braddock came to the colonies armed with comprehensive plans that included a campaign by provincials against the fort. It would not be until 1759, however, when the French were in retreat and had abandoned Fort St. Frédéric, that the British finally achieved their goal.

Those early 1755 plans died with Braddock in the wilderness of western Pennsylvania. The planned invasion of Lake Champlain stalled when Baron de Dieskau's French troops engaged William Johnson's provincials in the Battle of Lake George. Despite repelling the

Thomas Davies' drawing of the British camps at His Majesty's Fort at Crown Point after the French retreat in 1760. Courtesy Library of Congress.

Below, "A Plan of the Fort and Fortresses at Crown Point with their Environs…." The French fort (K) sits just to the right of the much larger Crown Point (A). The elaborate tree-lined avenues were never constructed. Courtesy Library of Congress.

Fort St. Frédéric as it probably looked in the 1740s. Its literally towering presence on the shore of Lake Champlain must have been an awe-inspiring sight to the Indians and a potent symbol of French power. Courtesy Crown Point SHS.

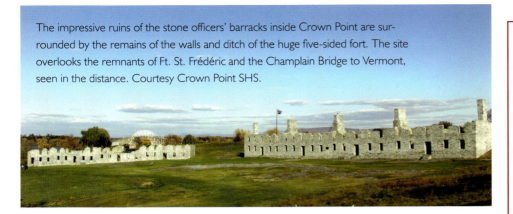

The impressive ruins of the stone officers' barracks inside Crown Point are surrounded by the remains of the walls and ditch of the huge five-sided fort. The site overlooks the remnants of Ft. St. Frédéric and the Champlain Bridge to Vermont, seen in the distance. Courtesy Crown Point SHS.

French and capturing de Dieskau, the Americans went into winter quarters rather than pursue the retreating French down the lake. Planned fulfillment of those efforts in 1756 disappeared with Montcalm's victory at Oswego and in the confusion of multiple changes of command. General Shirley, Braddock's replacement as commander of British forces, was himself replaced in June by the interim General Abercromby, who in turn was replaced by Lord Loudoun in July. Loudoun's imperious nature met stiff resistance from colonials determined to remain free from direct British military control, and that year's planned move on Fort St. Frédéric was abandoned. Further plans went unfulfilled in 1758 when Abercromby retreated after the disastrous infantry assault against the French *abatis* at Fort Carillon.

By 1759, however, French territory was shrinking as the French concentrated their forces for the defense of Montréal and Québec. Amherst, pushing north through the lakes with 11,300 men, encountered only token resistance at Fort Carillon before the French blew up the powder magazine and fled north, presumably, Amherst thought, to make a stand at Fort St. Frédéric. Surprised to discover that the French had tarried only long enough to blow up that fort as well, Amherst stopped to regroup and consolidate his forces in preparation for a final push in 1760. Having left work forces to reconstruct fortifications at Forts William Henry and Ticonderoga (as the British renamed Fort Carillon, giving it back its Mohawk name, Ticonderoga, "the place between the great waters"), Amherst ordered the construction of an entirely new fort near the site of the demolished Fort St. Frédéric. After serving as the staging area for General Haviland's 1760 advance on Montréal, Crown Point's military usefulness disappeared with the end of the war in 1763, and further construction ceased.

After a 1773 fire destroyed the main fort, the site changed hands several times during the American Revolution, providing cannon to Washington's army besieging Boston in 1775 and serving as a staging area for campaigns of both armies. ■ SB

- **VISITING CROWN POINT**
  Crown Point State Historic Site
  739 Bridge Road, Crown Point, NY 12928-2852 518-597-4666
  www.lakechamplainregion.com/cphistoricsite or www.nysparks.com
  • Open May to October; the Museum is open Wednesday through Monday (inclusive) from 9:00 a.m. until 5:00 p.m. and the grounds are open until dusk through Columbus Day.

Fusilier, Régiment de Berry 1758

France traditionally maintained a large army that fought in many European wars during the 17th and 18th centuries. The Seven Years' War kept most of France's army of over 200,000 men engaged in Western Europe, so relatively few forces could be spared for the defense of Canada. There were French troops from only 13 regular regiments serving in New France during the war. Defending the vast territories of New France spread available forces thin and there were few times that even 5,000 men could be assembled for any one campaign. The regulars formed a corps of highly-trained and disciplined troops, assisted by the *companies franche de la marine*, local militia, and depending on the year, varying numbers of Indian warriors.

The two battalions (over 1,000 men) of the Régiment de Berry that came to Canada in 1757 wore the standard regular infantry uniform — a heavy unbleached grey-white wool *justaucorps* coat with deep cuffs, dyed red for this unit. The regiment was part of the French force defending Fort Carillon in 1758 and was with Montcalm's army at Québec in 1759 and in Montréal in 1760. RT

Painting by Don Troiani, Historical Image Bank.

Resources for more information

Books, Audio Books, Video

A short and select listing of a few of the many thousands of useful and available sources

- A good place to start investigating the French & Indian War is either of Fred Anderson's two definitive works — *Crucible of War*, the most complete single-volume history, or *The War That Made America*, one-third as long but still comprehensive. *The War That Made America* is available as an unabridged audio book on 7 CDs, and there is also a 4-hour PBS Home Video version.
- Francis Jennings, *Empire of Fortune: Crowns, Colonies and Tribes in the Seven Years' War in America*
- Ruth Sheppard, ed., *Empires Collide: The French & Indian War, 1754-1763*, Oxford, UK, Osprey, 2006. A compendium of the various Osprey books covering the War
- Walter R. Borneman, *The French & Indian War: Deciding the Fate of North America*
- Seymour I. Schwartz, *The French and Indian War 1754-1763: The Imperial Struggle for North America* (profusely illustrated, and it's the illustrations that are the heart of this book)
- Beacock Fryer's 2 books — *Battlefields of Canada* and *More Battlefields of Canada* (both available in paperback)
- Fintan O'Toole, *White Savage: William Johnson and the Invention of America*
- John F. Ross, *War on the Run: The Epic Story of Robert Rogers and the Conquest of America's First Frontier*
- Ian Steele, *Betrayals: Fort William Henry & the "Massacre"*
- Mountain Lake PBS video, *The Forgotten War*, and an informative accompanying website www.pbsforgottenwar.org

Fiction

- James Fenimore Cooper, *The Last of the Mohicans* (book and movies)
- Kenneth Roberts, *Northwest Passage* (stirring account of the exploits of Major Robert Rogers — book and movie)
- Allan W. Eckert, *Wilderness Empire* (history disguised as fiction—fast-paced narrative, but a complete and accurate account)

Websites

- **Seaway Trail**
  http://www.seawaytrail.com/images/PDFs/STFrenchFactsSheet2009.pdf
- **Lakes to Locks Passage**
  http://www.lakestolocks.com/
- **Revolutionary Byway**
  http://www.adirondack.org/byways/bywayrevolutionary.php
- **New York State French and Indian War 250th Anniversary Commemoration Commission**
  http://www.fiw250.org/index.asp
- **America's Historic Lakes: The Lake Champlain and Lake George Historical Site**
  http://www.historiclakes.org/index.html
- **The Seven Years' War Timeline**
  http://www.ns1763.ca/remem/7yw-timeline-w.html
- **The Canadian Military History Gateway**
  http://cmhg.gc.ca/html/index-eng.asp
- **Dictionary of Canadian Biography**
  http://www.biographi.ca/index-e.html
- **A Set of Plans and Forts in America, 1765**
  http://www.masshist.org/maps/PlansandForts/intro.htm
- **The Seven Years' War Website**
  http://www.militaryheritage.com/7yrswar.htm
- **"The French and Indian War" at a website called Social Studies for Kids**
  http://www.socialstudiesforkids.com/articles/ushistory/frenchandindianwar1.htm
- **Illustrated Chronology of the Seven Years' War**
  http://web.archive.org/web/20050308115609/www.sevenyearswarassociation.com/Reference/ChronIntro.html
- **French and Indian War**
  http://www.frontierguard.org/Research/NJFG2A02.html
- **Adirondack History: French and Indian War**
  http://www.adirondack.net/history/french.asp
- **French and Indian War/Mohican History Links**
  http://www.mohicanpress.com/mo08021.html

A How-to Guide for Aspiring Reenactors

Interested in stepping back in time as a living history reenactor? Here are some ways to make your dream come true.

- Ask reenactors at French & Indian War, American Revolution, War of 1812 and other heritage events at historic sites about their clothing, weapons, tools, and equipment
- Contact reenactors and historic site managers about how you can join a living history unit
- Ask if units loan authentically-made uniforms and accoutrements for your first year or if they can provide patterns so you make your own
- Study the details of your chosen historic period to help you collect items true to that time by searching antiquarian book sales and eBay
- Ask unit leaders if they are strictly authentic or offer historically-sound commemoration; for example, some units camp primitive style and eat only the food of that era
- Be aware that joining a living history unit can be essential since participation at events is often by invitation only